Family Quarrels
in the Dutch Reformed Churches in the Nineteenth Century

The Pillar Church
Sesquicentennial Lectures

Robert P. Swierenga
Elton J. Bruins
A. C. Van Raalte Institute
Hope College

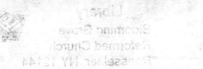

The Historical Series of the Reformed Church in America

No. 32

Family Quarrels
in the Dutch Reformed Churches in the Nineteenth Century

The Pillar Church
Sesquicentennial Lectures

Robert P. Swierenga
Elton J. Bruins
A. C. Van Raalte Institute
Hope College

Wm. B. Eerdmans Publishing Co.
Grand Rapids, Michigan

The Historical Series of the Reformed Church in America

This series has been inaugurated by the General Synod of the Reformed Church in America, acting through its Commission on History, for the purpose of encouraging historical research and providing a medium wherein this knowledge may be shared with the academic community and with the members of the denomination in order that a knowledge of the past may contribute to right action in the present.

General Editor

The Reverend Donald J. Bruggink, Ph.D.
Western Theological Seminary

Commission on History

Gerald F. De Jong, Ph.D., Orange City, Iowa
Sophie Mathonnet-Vander Well, M.Div., Pella, Iowa
Christopher Moore, New York, New York
Jennifer Reece, M.Div., Princeton, New Jersey
Jeffrey Tyler, Ph.D., Hope College, Holland, Michigan

To our grandchildren, the future of the church

Jacob, Trent, and Jillanne Greenhout
Sydney Swierenga
James, Katherine, and Thomas Plasman
Christopher Bruins

ISBN 0-8028-4709-9

Body text set in Adobe New Caledonia.
Chapter titles set in in Adobe Garamond.

In appreciation to

Peter H. Huizenga

Benefactor and Founder

of the A.C. Van Raalte Institute

Contents

Contents

Illustrations

xii

Tables and Figures

Acknowledgments

The authors contributed severally and jointly to the book. Robert P. Swierenga is primarily responsible for the introduction, chapters 1 and 3, bibliographic essay, the index, and illustrations; Elton J. Bruins is primarily responsible for chapters 2 and 4. Chapter 4, here revised, originally appeared in 1983 in *Perspectives on the Christian Reformed Church*, edited by Peter De Klerk and Richard R. De Ridder, and is used with permission of Baker Book House. The authors acknowledge their indebtedness to Elisabeth Dekker, former colleague at the A.C. Van Raalte Institute, for translations of primary sources; to Richard Harms, director of the Calvin College Archives, for research assistance and obtaining the photographs; to Larry J. Wagenaar, director of the Joint Archives of Holland, Hope College, for assistance in obtaining the photographs; and to Karen Schakel, administrative assistant at the A.C. Van Raalte Institute, for her careful proofreading and editorial assistance.

Preface

The Reverend Michael De Vries,
pastor of Pillar Church

As part of its sesquicentennial celebrations, Pillar Christian Reformed Church of Holland, Michigan, sponsored a lecture series in March of 1997 that focused on the religious history of the Dutch Calvinist immigration to West Michigan and the church struggles of the first settlers. One month earlier, on 9 February 1997, Pillar Church celebrated Dominie Albertus Van Raalte's founding of the town and church by holding a "Unity Service" with its long-estranged daughter congregation, First Reformed Church. I preached on the theme of "The Beauty of Unity," based on Psalm 133, and presented to the Reverend Daniel N. Gillett, pastor of First Reformed Church, a complete copy of the consistory minutes for the years 1850-1882, which include the years prior to the painful separation in 1882.

Despite an ardent desire for reconciliation in the Reformed community, this lecture series deals as much with divisions and strife as with unity. Every one of the pioneer pastors of the Holland colony—Albertus Van Raalte, Cornelius Vander Meulen, Marten Ypma, Seine Bolks, and Hendrik Klijn—were seceders from the Nederlands Hervormde Kerk (Reformed Church), the national church. If these leaders had not separated in 1834, there would have been no Holland colony to celebrate. Moreover, as I observed at the Unity service, while God does not condone divisions in the church God has blessed the local congregations and their respective denominations. One must also know that the founders, even when they disagreed, did so in the conviction that they were being obedient to God's Word.

We are pleased to give these fine lectures a wider audience. Becoming knowledgeable about these early struggles within the colony will help us understand the past and, hopefully, encourage us to go forward in faith and hope. We all live by grace!

Introduction

In Dutch Reformed circles certain dates resonate with meaning. Mention the year 1834 and the *Afscheiding* or "Secession" from *the Nederlands Hervormde Kerk* immediately comes to mind. This reformation movement, which harked back to the even more weighty years 1618-1619 (the Synod of Dort), gave birth to the Christian Seceded Church (*Christelijke Afgescheiden Kerk*) with its fervent spirit and stern orthodoxy. Seceder pastors and congregations led the emigration to North America in the 1840s and placed their stamp of pietism and reverence for Dortian polity on the immigrant churches of the Midwest.

The year 1857 similarly carries great emotional freight. It is the year of the second secession, when some 10 percent of the members of Classis Holland in western Michigan rejected the Union of 1850 with the Reformed Church in America (RCA) and founded the Christian Reformed Church in North America (CRC). The 1857 seceders were convinced that they were remaining true to the principles of 1834, whereas the 1850 unionists placed a higher value on the oneness of the visible body of Christ.

1

The seeds of 1857 were sown in 1834. Factions formed in the Christian Seceder Church between the Brummelkamp-Van Raalte party in the south and the de Cock-van Velzen party in the north. The ecumenical spirit of the south conflicted with the sterner Calvinism of the north. Both mindsets were carried in the religious and cultural baggage of the emigrants. Consequently, as the Reformed Church in America moved toward the American evangelical mainstream, the sterner Dortians withdrew and formed the Christian Reformed Church to maintain their revered religious heritage.

The third secession, in 1882, centered on this very issue of Americanization. Freemasonry, the quintessential American upper-class social organization, had made inroads among the leaders of the Reformed Church in the East, to the consternation of the midwestern immigrant churches. They had learned in the Netherlands to abhor freemasonry for its "pagan ceremonies" and beliefs grounded in the Enlightenment, although American Masonic lodges blended rather easily with mainstream Christianity. A majority of Van Raalte's own congregation, First Reformed Church (now Pillar Church), seceded in 1882, only six years after his death, and affiliated with the Christian Reformed Church two years later. The appeal of the junior denomination was its "Dutchness," upheld by the motto, "In isolation is our strength." This ideal guided it for several generations, until the influence of Abraham Kuyper's *Doleantie* movement gained a place among the leaders while the 1834 spirit waned among the laity.

The events of the years 1850, 1857, and 1882 made clear the divergent paths of the Dutch Reformed denominations in America. While the Reformed Church took its place in the American Protestant mainstream, the Christian Reformed Church resisted Americanization and tried to cling to its religious roots in the Netherlands. This allowed it to gather in the waves of immigrants from 1880 until World War I and again after World War II. This immigration has now ceased, and the Christian Reformed Church is rapidly adapting to the multiethnic American culture and the ecumenical spirit of American Protestantism.

This adaptation, which is inevitable and even necessary, together with the accelerated pace of secularization in all western societies since the 1960s, explains in part the turmoil and secessions that again plague the Christian Reformed Church. Since 1990 more than 30,000 people, about 10 percent of the membership, has withdrawn, transferred out, or seceded to form new associations and alliances. This loss rate is the same proportion that initially seceded from Classis Holland of the Reformed Church in 1857 to form the Christian Reformed Church.

This fledgling body struggled for a decade or more before a flood of new immigrants secured its survival after the Civil War ended. The key to enfolding most of the newcomers in its congregations was the condemnation by the mother church in the Netherlands of the Reformed Church in America because of its acquiescence to Freemasonry. This emotional issue has its counterpart today in the decision of the Christian Reformed Church to ordain women as elders and pastors. A potentially more devastating issue, that of accepting practicing homosexuals as members in good standing in the churches, which has been considered in several classical assemblies, would greatly accelerate the loss rate and hasten the formation of seceder denominations. In a real way, the Dutch Reformed communities today are reliving the struggles of the pioneer generation 150 years ago to maintain a pure church.

No one has yet studied the religious mentality of the 30,000 departed Christian Reformed members of the 1990s. Their reasons for leaving are varied and complex. A few left, in fact, because the pace of modernization was too slow! But judging from numerous writings by seceder leaders in the periodical press, letters by lay people to editors of church papers, and comments of elders and pastors at church assemblies, those separating from the CRC share the mindset of the 1834 and 1857 seceders. These dissenters actually included at least two camps, the individualistic pietists (who worshiped in lay conventicles) and the stern Calvinists of the northern Netherlands who valued the Dortian church order and the three historic Reformed creeds.

The Christian Seceded Church of 1834 managed to hold these diverse factions together through compromise and accommodation. The Christian Reformed Church in North America had done the same for more than one hundred years. But the consensus has broken down. Today, the pietists in the CRC are gravitating to the experiential American denominations— Wesleyan Methodists, Assemblies of God, Peoples Churches, Baptists, and nondenominational megachurches. The sterner Calvinists, on the other hand, are seceding to form orthodox congregations modeled after the "original" Christian Reformed churches of the pre-World War II era, complete with the 1934 or 1959 *Psalter Hymnal*, weekly catechetical preaching, regular family visits, and care for discipline. The pietists stand in the tradition of the Brummelkamp-Van Raalte wing of the Afscheiding, and the orthodox hark back to the de Cock-van Velzen wing. The Kuyperians in the CRC have generally stood firm and are the backbone of the denomination today.

It is the authors' hope and prayer that this book will remind the Dutch-born Reformed churches of their rich religious heritage that our ancestors defended against bitter assault and preserved with blood. It was a history of factiousness and strife, but also of deep piety, love for Christ's church, defense of biblical truth, and bold action to work out the faith in "world and life."

I
1834
Afscheiding and Emigration

Importance of the Afscheiding Emigration to America

The founding pastors of the Holland colony—Van Raalte, Vander Meulen, Ypma, Bolks, and Klijn—were seceders from the Hervormde Kerk. If there had been no Afscheiding in 1834, life among the Dutch immigrants in America would have been markedly different. First, without the religious motive fewer families would have left the homeland. The Dutch never caught America fever like the Irish or Germans. They loved their *gezelligheid* and believed in the adage: "Oost, West, T'huis Best." The Netherlands ranked only tenth among European nations in the extent of emigration. Had there been no religious turmoil and persecution, the overall Dutch emigration might have been reduced up to 25 percent—75,000 people.

Some 13,000 Seceders emigrated between 1845 and 1880, mostly in the first wave of the 1840s. The earlier an emigration tradition began in a particular Dutch village, the more emigrants left from that village over the decades. The fact that the Seceders left in such large numbers in the first years thus had a multiplier effect on the total emigration. Many Hervormde Kerk members and even Catholics decided to follow the example of the Seceders, who first made migration a normal response to the diminished future at home. Emigration became the thing to do among the distressed *kleine luyden*.

Second, and most important, the Seceder dominies organized and led the initial exodus, in order to establish colonies where the believers could live together and not be scattered and likely lost to the faith. Eight Calvinist colonies were founded before 1860, and more than one hundred by 1900. The colonies acted as magnets, attracting members of the Hervormde Kerk and other splinter groups as well. Herbert Brinks estimates that between 1846 and 1900 three-quarters of all Dutch emigrants settled in Reformed enclaves.[1] These people, of course, experienced a much slower and less intense Americanization process than the non-enclaved emigrants. The ethnic cohesion in the colonies and their continuing ties to the mother churches preserved the Dutch Reformed identity for many generations. In 1920 there were more than five hundred Christian Reformed and Reformed congregations in the United States, many still worshiping in the Dutch language.

Ironically, as Brinks noted, by colonizing, the Seceders "who had been marginalized in their native villages became dominant in their transplanted settlements," where they "assumed a cultural authority that was much like that of the national church they had spurned in 1834." They wanted to preserve old values and practices and to remain "more Dutch than the Dutch."[2]

The Seceders were the most focused of all Dutch emigrants. They left in the largest proportions and almost all settled in colonies. In 1849 Seceders numbered a little more than 1 percent of the Dutch population, yet they contributed 65 percent of all emigrants from the Netherlands in the peak years of Seceder emigration—1846 through 1849. In 1847, when the colonies of Holland and Zeeland (Michigan), Pella (Iowa), South Holland (Illinois), and Sheboygan (Wisconsin) were founded, Seceders made up 79 percent of all emigrants (see table). In the years 1846-1849, 80 of every 1000 Seceders in the Netherlands emigrated, compared to only 4 per 1000 among

1   Herbert Brinks, ed. *Dutch American Voices: Letters from the United States, 1850-1930* (Ithaca, N.Y.: Cornell University Press, 1995), 2-3.
2   Brinks, *Dutch American Voices*, 15, 11.

Hervormde Kerk adherents. Fully 60 percent of all Seceder emigrants to America in the entire period 1835-1880 left between 1847 and 1857. The intense and focused migration of this religious minority, therefore, gave it a presence in the Midwest that far exceeded its numbers.

Table 1.1: *Emigration by Year, Hervormde Kerk and Afscheiding Kerk Members, 1835-1857*

Year	Hervormde Kerk+		Afscheiding Kerk°		Total
	N	%	N	%	N
1835-44	152	61	99	39	251
1845	210	49	216	51	426
1846	349	27	957	73	1306
1847	835	21	3223	79	4058
1848	837	52	779	48	1616
1849	1006	59	691	41	1697
1850	333	81	77	19	410
1851	565	83	118	17	683
1852	764	93	60	7	824
1853	801	84	152	16	953
1854	2457	86	402	14	2859
1855	1376	80	342	20	1718
1856	1300	81	311	19	1611
1857	1191	89	142	11	1333
Totals	12176	62	7569	38	19745

+ Includes 285 *Nederduits Hervormden*, 3 Presbyterian *Hervormden*, 13 *Waals Hervormden*, and 4 English *Hervormden*.

° Includes 4,526 *Christelijke Afgescheidenen*, 2,580 *Gereformeerden*, 452 *Hervormde Afgescheiden*, 6 *Christelijke Gereformeerden*, 4 *Waals Gereformeerden*, and 1 English *Gereformeerden*.

Source: Robert P. Swierenga, comp., *Dutch Emigrants to the United States, South Africa, South America, and Southeast Asia, 1835-1880: An Alphabetical Listing by Household Heads and Independent Persons* (Wilmington, Del.: Scholarly Resources, 1983); augmented for the years 1831-1847 with data from the report of the Department of Binnenlandsche Zaken, "Staat van landverhuizers 1831-1847," *Nederlandsche Staatscourant*, 5 September 1848, 2.

National Synod of Dordrecht, 1618-1619

Emigrants from the Hervormde Kerk outnumbered Seceders in every year except 1845, 1846, and 1847. Hervormden made up 58 percent of all Dutch emigrants in the period 1835-1880, compared to the Seceders' 20 percent. Many Hervormden joined the Seceder colonies but others scattered far and wide, often choosing the cities, where they quickly assimilated; some 10 percent even settled in the Dutch East Indies and other parts of the world. So the Hervormde Kerk immigrants must not be ignored—they outnumbered Seceders two to one—but Seceders deserve the top billing when we think about the founding of the Dutch Calvinist colonies in America.

Antecedents to the Afscheiding—Rational Religion

The golden age of the Dutch national church was the century following the Synod of Dort (1618-1619), the historic assembly which consolidated the gains of the Protestant Reformation in the Netherlands by promulgating a new creed—the Canons of Dort, and a new church order—the Articles of

Bishop Simon Episcopius before the Dordrecht Synod

Dort, both of which the orthodox viewed as divinely inspired and the final word on all issues. The Dutch Calvinists came to consider themselves as the new Israel, a chosen people under God, country, and the house of Orange. But the desire to continue reforming doctrine and life soon waned, and church leaders began to accept rationalist thinking, which viewed the Bible and the three Reformed forms of unity as man-made creeds. This declension prompted conservative teachers, later revered as the "Old Writers," to publish doctrinal compendiums of the way of faith that stressed experiential knowledge rather than mere head knowledge. They also wrote practical handbooks for religious life, describing how to be Reformed in everyday life as fishermen, farmers, shopkeepers, or housewives. But it was a losing cause, because the national church was too weak ecclesiastically to discipline leaders with heterodox beliefs. Indeed, two hundred years passed before the church convened another synod.[3]

3 Gerrit J. tenZythoff, *Sources of the Secession: The Netherlands Hervormde Kerk on the Eve of the Dutch Immigration to the Midwest* (Grand Rapids: Wm. B. Eerdmans, 1987), 103-104.

By the early nineteenth century the spirit of toleration of Enlightenment thought had gained the upper hand theologically, and the government interfered more and more in church polity. The signs that the spiritual leaders "had fallen asleep" were everywhere.[4] Few protested when Napoleon's revolutionary army came into the Netherlands in 1795 and purged traditional Calvinism from public life. Almost the first act of the secular "Patriotten," the Orange-Democrats, as the liberal democrats were called, was to disestablish the national church and place all religions on an equal footing at law. Under the banner of nonsectarianism, public funds were cut off to pay pastor's salaries and the teaching of Reformed doctrine in the public schools was replaced with deistic religion. Furthermore, the Education Law of 1806 took from private Reformed schools the right to use doctrinal criteria in hiring new teachers.[5]

National Synod of 1816

The crowning blow came after the restoration of the House of Orange, when the monarch became the highest authority in the church. In 1815 King Willem I convened a national synod, the first since 1618, and rather than allow the normal procedure of election by provincial assemblies, he hand-picked delegates who reflected the modern temper.[6] With little debate, the synod made a number of momentous changes that threatened completely to undo the Hervormde Kerk. Most importantly, the synod altered the Form of Subscription ever so slightly and thus made its meaning ambiguous. The new oath allowed candidates to accept the doctrines of the three official creeds "in so far as" (rather than "because") they agreed with Scripture. This subjective clause allowed pastors and professors the liberty to interpret official doctrines as they saw fit, which emasculated the creedal foundation of the church and protected those who denied the Trinity and other vital

4 TenZythoff, *Sources of the Secession*, 17-42; Henry E. Dosker, *Levenschets van Rev. A.C. van Raalte, D.D.* (Nijkerk: C. C. Callenbach, 1893), 7. An English translation by Elisabeth Dekker is available at the A. C. Van Raalte Institute, Holland, Mich.
5 TenZythoff, *Sources of Secession*, 1-24.
6 TenZythoff, *Sources of Secession*, 25-42; Albertus Pieters, "Historical Introduction," in *Classis Holland Minutes, 1848-1858* (Grand Rapids: Wm. B. Eerdmans, 1950), 10-12. See also J. Vree, "De Nederlandse Hervormde Kerk in de jaren voor de Afscheiding," in *De Afscheiding van 1834 en haar geschiedenis*, ed. W. Bakker, O. J. de Jong, W. van't Spijker, L. J. Wolthuis (Kampen: J. H. Kok, 1984), 30-61.

Willem I, King of the Netherlands

teachings.[7] The synod also dropped the requirement of weekly catechetical preaching.

Most importantly, the synod changed church polity by creating a standing executive committee to run the church and by making delegates to all classes and synods royal appointees. Instead of the revered Dortian polity, the national church now became virtually an administrative arm of the state.

The king by royal decree on 7 January 1816 promulgated the Church Order of 1816 as the ecclesiastical law of the land. With this act, the Hervormde Kerk was reestablished as the only state-supported religious body and public monies again flowed to support it, but it was no longer

7   The phrases "in so far as" and "because" are Kampen professor Helenius's de Cock's gloss on the 1816 formulary in his booklet, *The Secession in the Netherlands* (Kampen: S. van Velzen, Jr., 1866), 10. An English translation by John C. Verbrugge is available in the Calvin College Archives, Grand Rapids, Mich.. The actual change in the oath was more subtle. The 1618 formulation stated that the three forms of unity were "in all things in agreement with God's Word." The 1816 formulation did not specify the three doctrinal standards, but instead referred to "the doctrine which in harmony with God's Holy Word is contained in the accepted formulas." The ambiguous phrase "accepted formulas" allowed candidates to reject the Canons of Dort, the standard of Calvinist orthodoxy.

Presbyterian in form, with authority flowing upward from the local congregations. Rather, power flowed from the top down, and the church shared with the government the task of nurturing loyal subjects. Given the ever closer bond between church and state, this change meant that any future church conflict would inevitably become a threat to the political order. In one stroke the king undermined the historic national church and, in the opinion of reformers, further weakened the church and the nation.[8]

Conventicles

The king's arbitrary actions aroused very little public dissent. Most clergy were happy to get paid regularly again and their parishioners welcomed the restoration of the national church, even if it was subject to closer government control. Opposition against the new regime came only from a few orthodox local congregations and a small group of intellectuals.

In the countryside, passive resistance arose when the first national synod to meet under the revised structure **mandated** pastors in each worship service to select one or more hymns from the new hymnal, called *De Evangelische Gezangen*, which included 192 gospel songs to augment the traditional Genevan psalms. The synod had adopted this hymnal in 1807 and recommended it to the churches but did not make its use obligatory. When that changed in 1816, some "stijf kops" refused to sing the "man-made songs," which they thought smacked of Arminianism. They stood silently, or put on their caps, or even marched out of the church until the singing was over. A few sympathetic ministers defied the ruling and selected only the psalms, but they were subject to discipline.[9]

In the next years pious members of the national church simply walked away from it and turned to the traditional conventicles (*gezelschappen*),

---

8 The Hervormde Kerk and the national government had been cozy since the rise of the Orange monarchy, which was based on the Constantinian idea of the two kingdoms working together in harmony. But the royal decree undermined this arrangement by subordinating God's kingdom to Caesar's kingdom. The law also required that all public officials must be church members, thus making it impossible to discipline those enlightened aristocrats who neglected worship, lived scandalously, or were free thinkers. Dosker, "Life of Van Raalte," p. 7, 12, 14-15; tenZythoff, *Sources of Secession*, 35-39, 43-45; Pieters, "Historical Introduction," 12.

9 Pieters, "Historical Introduction," 11-12; Jeanne M. Jacobson, Elton J. Bruins, Larry Wagenaar, *Albertus C. Van Raalte: Dutch Leader and American Patriot* (Holland, Mich.: Hope College, 1996), 93-98.

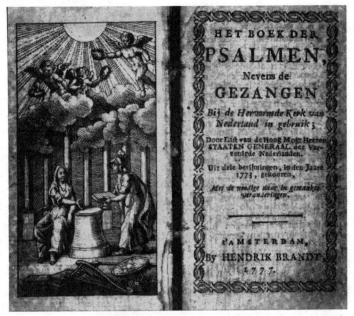

Official Dutch Psalter of 1777

extra-church assemblies of the devout that had arisen at the first signs of
apostasy in the national church in the decades after Dort. Here people
practiced the community of the saints, testified to the inner workings of the
Holy Spirit, and warned against false teachers. The nineteenth century
conventicles evolved into full-fledged worship services held in homes and
barns where elders read sermons of the Old Writers. Recognized local
groups were the Zwijndrecht Newlights of Stoffel Müller (1816), the
followers of the prophet Jan Mazereeuw of West Friesland (1824), and the
Restored Church of Christ of Johan Vijgeboom in Zeeland (1823).[10]

Réveil

Opposition also formed among a few ministers and intellectuals in the
major universities, including Leiden, which was the major Reformed

10 TenZythoff, *Sources of Secession*, 45-48; Jacob van Hinte, *Netherlanders in
America: A Study of Emigration and Settlement in the Nineteenth and Twentieth
Centuries in the United States of America* (1928), ed. Robert P. Swierenga, trans.
Adriaan de Wit (Grand Rapids: Baker Book House, 1985), 88-89.

Seceder "House Church"

academy and theological school. At Leiden, Rev. Nicolaas Schotsman (1754-1822), a minister of the Hervormde Kerk, first raised a lone voice of protest. He was influenced by the religious revival (or *Réveil*) that began in Geneva, Switzerland, around 1810.[11] When Schotsman in 1819 memorialized the Synod of Dort in two published sermons, liberal clerics counterattacked viciously. This, in turn, aroused Willem Bilderdijk (1756-1832), a noted lawyer and the founding teacher of a private theological school at Leiden, to rise to the defense of Schotsman as one truly warring for Jesus Christ.

Bilderdijk's teaching and pamphlet war against unbelief earned him the title of the father of the Dutch *Réveil*. His major disciples, the political leader Guillaume Groen van Prinsterer (1801-1876) and the Portuguese Jewish converts Isaac da Costa (1798-1860) and Abraham Capadose (1795-1874), also engaged in the battle for truth. These men defended the Bible and the Reformed creeds and brought the spiritual awakening at Geneva to the Netherlands.[12] The *Réveil* sparked a spirit of renewal and piety in

11 M. Elisabeth Kluit, *Het Protestantse* Réveil *in Nederland en daarbuiten, 1815-1865* (Amsterdam: H. J. Paris, 1970).

12 Vree, "Nederlandse Hervormde Kerk," 47-52. Bilderdijk's students, da Costa, Groen van Prinsterer, Capadose, and Willem de Clercq, became known as the "Haagse Heeren," because they later assumed leading positions in the government.

Willem Bilderdijk

Isaac da Costa

Abraham Capadose

Guillaume Groen van Prinsterer

Reformed circles and made resistance to rationalistic thinking and doctrinal heterodoxy intellectually respectable.

In addition to Bilderdijk's defense of traditional Reformed teachings, he also espoused the new millennial beliefs that the end of the world was near and that the House of Orange and the Hervormde Kerk would play a crucial role as history reached its climax. In a similar vein, he and Capadose, a medical doctor, opposed the government-mandated smallpox vaccinations for school children. Virtually all the Seceder clerics later adopted this same anti-vaccination position, which caused their children to be barred from school.[13]

13 TenZythoff, *Sources of Secession*, 73-76; also 85-91, 105-109. Interestingly, Bilderdijk was premillenarian in his thinking while da Costa was postmillenarian, as was Hofstede de Groot, the leader of the Groninger *Réveil* School. Cf. Lubbertus Oostendorp, *H.P. Scholte: Leader of the Secession of 1834 and Founder of Pella* (Franeker: T. Wever, 1964), 32-33. Compulsory vaccinations for children began under a Napoleonic law of 1807. For an analysis of the Secession through the eyes of leaders in the Christian Reformed Church who find modern-day parallels in their own protest movement, see *The Reformation of 1834: Essays in Commemoration of the Act of Secession and Return*, ed. Peter Y. De Jong and Nelson Kloosterman (Orange City, Ia: Pluim Publishing, 1984).

Petrus Hofstede de Groot

Secession in 1834—Links to Réveil

The *Réveil* men did not break with the Hervormde Kerk, but their stress on a religion of the heart and their radical eschatological expectations strongly influenced the Seceder leaders Hendrik de Cock (1801-1842), Hendrik P. Scholte (1806-1868), and Albertus C. Van Raalte (1811-1876).

The links between the *Réveil* and the Secession of 1834 were forged in the theological schools at two universities, Groningen and Leiden. At Groningen Professor Petrus Hofstede de Groot (1802-1886) and two colleagues rejected the popular rationalistic theology and emphasized the importance of the heart in Christian belief. This became known as the Groninger theology. In an unusual gesture, the Groninger professors opened their lectures to local pastors and thus spread widely their warm and experiential Christianity.

Hendrik de Cock of Ulrum: Father of the Afscheiding

Hofstede de Groot's best friend at the university was his fellow theology student Hendrik de Cock. When Hofstede de Groot took a professorship at Groningen in 1829 and gave up his pastorate of the Hervormde Kerk at Ulrum, de Cock replaced him in the pulpit, and his friend preached the

Calvin College Archives

Hendrik de Cock

sermon at the installation. Soon, de Cock's devout parishioners pushed him to reexamine historic Calvinism and he read Calvin's *Institutes of the Christian Religion* for the first time. In amazement, de Cock came to understand that salvation was entirely a gift of God's grace and that a person, even with a keen mind and university education, could do nothing to earn it.[14]

When the Belgian revolt against Dutch rule began in 1830, de Cock preached that God was punishing the nation for departing from God's ways. He also published his views in a popular pamphlet. He would be a watchman to "blow the trumpet to warn the people" of the wrath to come. The public response was overwhelming. De Cock had touched a nerve, and people flocked to Ulrum by the thousands to hear him. But his erstwhile friend

14 TenZythoff, *Sources of Secession*, 104-110; P.N. Holtrop, "De Afscheiding— breekpunt en kristallisatiepunt," in *De Afscheiding van 1834 en haar geschiedenis*, 62-99; Herbert J. Brinks, "De Afscheiding—1834-1984," *Origins* 2, no. 2 (1984): 24-26. A brief popular account of de Cock is I. Van Dellen, *The Secession of 1834: A Reformation Movement* (Grand Rapids: Wm. B. Eerdmans, 1934). The best biography is J.A. Wormser, *Een Schat in aarden vaten*, Vol. III, "Werken zoolang het dag is: "Het leven van Hendrik de Cock* (Nijverdal: E.J. Bosch, 1915).

Nederlands Hervormde   *Pulpit of Nederlands Hervormde*
Kerk, Ulrum   *Kerk, Ulrum*

Hofstede de Groot condemned his new views as too radical. Read the Bible and John Calvin, de Cock thundered in reply. The friendship was doomed.

De Cock preached boldly from his pulpit in Ulrum, and many parents, who believed their own preachers were unconverted, beseeched him to baptize their children. Scholte, pastor of the Hervormde Kerk at Doeveren in Noord Brabant, counseled him not to violate Reformed principles and baptize children of nonmembers, but de Cock did so anyway. This sparked official action; the Classis of Middelstum instituted formal proceedings against him.

De Cock then lambasted two clerical critics by name in a pamphlet (entitled *Defense of True Reformed Doctrine and of the True Reformed Believers*). He charged that his colleagues were "two wolves in the sheep-fold who can preach much better about eating and drinking, nice weather and long days, about gardening and farming, about newspapers and war, than about the Kingdom of Heaven, as they lead the way for their congregations to the markets and horse races, drinking and singing until early dawn, or attending meetings for the so-called [society for the] common

Nederlands Hervormde Kerk, Ulrum

good."[15] De Cock also wrote a pamphlet attacking hymns as "contrary to the word of God" and "a concoction of siren lovesongs fit to draw the Reformed believers away from the saving doctrine."[16] He certainly had a way with words!

Despite an immediate suspension and the start of proceedings to depose him, de Cock was determined to remain in the national church and reform it from within. But events soon forced him to withdraw. In October 1834 Scholte traveled to Ulrum in a show of support. When the news spread of Scholte's coming, thousands of people gathered to hear him preach. At a Friday evening service at Ulrum, Scholte castigated unfaithful ministers as "idolaters and prophets of deceit" and fervently proclaimed the Reformed faith. Classis Middelstum was not pleased. When Scholte asked to preach again at the Sunday afternoon service, the classis ordered its supervisor not to allow it. The supervisor delivered the decision at the church door before a large crowd, at which some men roughed him up and the police closed the

15 Van Hinte, *Netherlanders in America*, 90.
16 TenZythoff, *Sources of Secession*, 117-125.

Parsonage of Nederlands Hervormde Kerk, Ulrum

church to avoid a riot. That night Scholte preached in an outdoor service and then left Ulrum immediately.

The following Monday, 13 October 1834, de Cock presented to his consistory a document, the "Act of Secession and Return," which he and the entire consistory signed. He explained: "Everything now fitted together for me as if it were an indication of the Lord what I had to do and which way I had to go." The state church appeared to him to be apostate, showing few marks of the true church. The next evening the congregation met, and 137 members also signed the document. The Ulrum church had sparked the secession of 1834. Thereafter de Cock became a "home missionary," planting numerous churches throughout the provinces of Groningen and Drenthe. Within a year sixteen churches had been organized in the north. Scholte was suspended from his pulpit two weeks after de Cock's secession, and 287 members of his congregations at Doeveren and Genderen withdrew with him.[17] The reformation of the Dutch Calvinist church was now underway.

17 Quotes in De Jong and Kloosterman, *Reformation of 1834*, 28, and tenZythoff, *Sources of Secession*, 125-127. For the Secession statement of the Ulrum consistory, signed by seventy men, see Oostendorp, *Scholte*, 57, which also describes in detail the secession in Ulrum and Doeveren and Genderen, 57-63.

Hendrik P. Scholte

The Scholte Club at the University of Leiden

The second seat of secession developed around the *Réveil* group at Leiden University in the 1820s. In 1829, Scholte enrolled there as a student in the theological school and soon became friends of Bilderdijk and da Costa and joined the movement. After his two mentors died in 1831, Scholte gathered around him a group of five younger orthodox students of theology to form the so-called Scholte Club, which included Anthony Brummelkamp (1811-1888), Simon van Velzen (1809-1896), Albertus Van Raalte (these three later married de Moen sisters and became brothers-in-law), Louis Bähler (1766-1838), and Georg Gezelle Meerburg (1806-1855). It is remarkable that the oldest university of Holland should train all the leading Seceder dominies except de Cock. The youthfulness of these "soldiers of the cross" is also noteworthy. The average age in 1834 was twenty-six years; Scholte was oldest at twenty-nine, and Van Raalte and Brummelkamp were youngest at only twenty-three.

The professors at Leiden were not happy with the Scholte Club. The rebel students often skipped the faculty lectures and rather repaired to the

Anthony Brummelkamp

Simon van Velzen

Georg Gezelle Meerburg

Albertus C. Van Raalte

living room of a pious old grain merchant named Johannes le Féburé, who taught them the Bible and the Reformed faith[18]. This made Scholte and his followers marked men, but all except Van Raalte were able to graduate in the years 1832-1834 and enter the pulpit before church authorities could marshall their forces. Van Raalte had the misfortune to graduate last, in 1835, and his road was blocked by professors and church officials who refused to recommend him for candidacy. So Van Raalte alone joined the dissenting church without first being deposed or resigning his pulpit in the Hervormde Kerk. This rejection was the more hurtful because Van Raalte had a strong desire to remain in the church in which his father had been a pastor.

Thus, the protest movement came to a head in 1834-1835 and gained a name, the *Afscheiding*, under the leadership of de Cock in Groningen,

18 Oostendorp, *Scholte*, 37-48.

Scholte in Utrecht and Noord Brabant, Brummelkamp in Gelderland, Van
Raalte in Overijssel, van Velzen in Friesland, and Gezelle Meerburg in
Noord Brabant. Later associates were Huibert J. Budding(h) (1810-1870)
and Cornelius Vander Meulen (1800-1876) in Zeeland, Lambertus G.
Ledeboer (1806-1863) in Zuid Holland, and H. Jöffers (1808-1874) in
Groningen, among others.[19] In 1836 Scholte took the initiative and called
the leaders to convene at Amsterdam for the first synod. The body of five
ministers and eleven elders examined Van Raalte and admitted him to the
ministry and petitioned the king for religious liberty, but differences of
opinion on church order questions hampered the synod. At the 1837
meeting, the body adopted a new church order written by Scholte, but the
churches in the south rejected it. They formed their own denomination in
1844, the Reformed Churches Under the Cross (*Gereformeerde Kerken
onder het kruis*), and reaffirmed their commitment to the Dort church
order. It was 1869 before the two factions joined together again.

Official Persecution

The king responded to the Seceders' request for recognition by condemning
the unauthorized meetings and demanding that they dissolve their
organization, obey the law, and submit to the "established and recognized
church." The argument was that the separatists were harming the church by
arousing suspicion against pastors and causing a steep drop in attendance
and contributions for the church and deacons' funds. On 5 July 1836 the king
issued a royal decree denouncing the Seceders as schismatics, fomenters of
unrest, and secret agitators (*scheurmakers, onruststokers en geheime
opruijers*).

However, the king also opened the door a crack, allowing individual
congregations to assemble, provided their gatherings did not have the
"signs, the form, and the appearance" of regular worship services, i.e., no
sacraments, no ministerial title, and no black coat with tails. A policeman

19 J.A. Wormser, *Een Schat in aarden vaten*, vol. 1, *In twee werelddeelen: Het leven
  van Albertus Christiaan van Raalte* (Nijverdal: E.J. Bosch, 1915); vol. 2, *"Door
  kwaar gerucht en goed gerucht:" Het leven van Hendrik Peter Scholte* (Nijverdal:
  E.J. Bosch, 1915); vol. 4, *Karacter en genade: Het leven van Simon van Velzen*
  (Nijverdal: E.J. Bosch, 1915); J.C. Rullmann, vol. 5, *Ernst en vrede: Het leven van
  Georg Frans Gezelle Meerburg* (Baarn: E.J. Bosch, 1919). The best genealogical
  study of the numerous Afscheiding leaders, with an excellent historical-sociological
  introduction by editor Theo N. Schelhaas, is *De afscheidenen van 1834 en hun
  nageslacht* (Kampen: J.H. Kok, 1984).

would stand at the door to ensure compliance. Most Seceders were not of a mind to accept this humiliating offer. Van Raalte, who was pastoring the church at Genemuiden, declared at the city hall that he would never comply with these rules or give up his title as a servant of God, and then he left in a "big huff, swinging his three corner hat."[20]

The decision of the king and his officials to suppress the free church movement was not only ill-advised but unconstitutional. Scholte, in a letter to the king, appealed to the Constitution of 1814, which specifically granted freedom of religion and the equal right of all religious faiths to carry on their worship in public. But the liberal church leaders did not want religious freedom for the orthodox separatists, and they prevailed on the king not to honor the freedom of conscience clause in the fundamental document.[21]

Government officials moved to quell the separatist movement by expelling the rebel clerics and imposing heavy fines and even jail terms for their civil disobedience.[22] Scholte and de Cock were given eighteen-month jail sentences in 1834 for the ruckus at Ulrum, but both were released on bond after several days. Van Raalte spent twelve days in jail in 1837. By misusing an old Napoleonic statute that forbade regular public assemblies of more than twenty persons for religious, political, or literary purposes without official permission, the government levied fines of f100 ($40) on clerics every time they conducted an unauthorized worship service.[23] In four years

20 J. Weitkamp, "De vervolgingen," in *"Van scheurmakers, onruststokers en geheime opruijers..."*: *De Afscheiding in Overijssel*, ed. Freerk Pereboom, H. Hille, and H. Reenders (Kampen: Uitgave IJsselakademie, 1984), 246, 255-257, 264. An English translation of pages 198-301 by Elisabeth Dekker is available at the A. C. Van Raalte Institute. The Royal Decree of 5 July 1836 was a detailed response to the Seceder petition.

21 Oostendorp, *Scholte*, 64-65, 88-89.

22 It was illegal to conduct unauthorized worship services with more than twenty persons, ten Zythoff, *Sources of Secession*, 48-49. The best study of the persecution in Overijssel is H. Reenders, "Albertus C. van Raalte als leider van Overijsselse Afgescheiden," in *"Van scheurmakers, onruststokers en geheime opruijers..."*: *De Afscheiding in Overijssel*, 98-197.

23 Henry S. Lucas, *Netherlanders in America: Dutch Immigration and Settlement to the United States and Canada, 1789-1950* (Ann Arbor: University of Michigan Press, 1955; reprint, Grand Rapids: Wm. B. Eerdmans, 1989), 42-53; Henry Beets, *Life and Times of Jannes Van de Luyster, Founder of Zeeland, Michigan* (Zeeland, Mich.: Zeeland Record Company, 1949), 12. TenZythoff, *Sources of Secession*, 49, quotes in English translation the relevant articles 291, 292, 294 of the Napoleonic Code.

Huibert J. Budding

of preaching throughout the islands of Walcheren and Zuid-Beveland, Budding was fined more than f40,000 ($16,000). Counting it a joy to suffer for Christ, he refused to pay the fines and spent seven months in jail before the king pardoned him. Van Raalte's fines also totaled about f40,000 for his preaching throughout the province of Overijssel.[24]

Consistory members were fined f50 ($20) each per service, and owners of a house or barn used for worship had to pay f100. Jannes Vande Luyster (1789-1862), the founder of Zeeland, Michigan, and an elder in the Seceder church in Borssele, was fined repeatedly as an elder and for allowing the use of his barn.[25] Despite fines totaling in the hundreds of thousands of guilders and the deployment of thousands of troops to break up the illegal worship services, which the government defined as "riots," the Seceder clerics and elders carried on, preaching to as many as one thousand spiritually thirsty people at a time in open air worship services.

24 Lucas, *Netherlanders in America*, 119-120, 52. On Budding's checkered career, see Herbert J. Brinks, "Father Budding, 1810-1870," *Origins* 14, no. 2 (1986): 19-23.
25 Beets, *Van de Luyster*, 12-16.

All of the preachers served numerous congregations in their provinces as itinerants, until more men could be apprenticed in parsonages and trained in Seceder theological schools to fill the pulpits. The Seceder preachers tried to avoid the police by assembling in groups of twenty or less, or they fled the jurisdiction immediately after the service, keeping one step ahead of the law. They would obey God rather than misguided government officials. No wonder that in America Van Raalte cherished freedom of religion as such a precious right!

The official persecution was relatively short-lived, as one would expect in the generally tolerant Netherlands, and the intensity varied from province to province and even city to city. The government also learned that it was not only very costly but also impossible to stifle the devout believers, who declared that the government would have to ban them from the Fatherland or behead them to stop them. Quartering of soldiers in homes of dissidents was stopped in 1837, no Seceders were jailed after 1839, and soldiers did not break up Seceder meetings after 1840. But fines continued to be levied in scattered places until 1846, particularly in the province of Utrecht.

Beginning in 1838, the "illegal" Seceder congregations began applying for legal status, which the government first allowed in 1836 under certain conditions. They must submit a petition for freedom of assembly, which admits to their former illegal behavior (thus making them admit to being a false church); renounce their place in the national church (when they really desired to reform it from within); agree to take care of their own poor and be entirely self-supporting; formulate a new church order other that of Dort; and promise to submit to the government.

Scholte in 1838 was the first to accept the stringent terms and write a freedom petition for his Utrecht congregation. The civil government approved, and he adopted the name "Christian Seceded Church," since the law forbade the use of the title Reformed. Scholte's unilateral action broke the Seceders' "united front" against the government and prompted several other churches to petition for recognition, including congregations Van Raalte had planted at Genemuiden, Ommen, and Den Ham (1839).[26] Most Seceder congregations refused on principle to "sell out" to the government and thereby deny their holy calling to reform the national church. They remained subject to prosecution.

---

26 Reenders, "Van Raalte als leider van Overijssele Afgescheidenen," 145-146.

After Willem I abdicated the throne in 1840, King Willem II further softened the religious oppression, and the new constitution of 1848 guaranteed complete religious freedom. It was 1870, however, before the government officially recognized the Christian Seceded Church and allowed them to use the name Reformed (*Gereformeerd*).

By 1849, forty thousand people (1.3 percent of the population) belonged to the Christian Seceded Church, and the Hervormde Kerk had lost 5 percent of its members. There were many more sympathizers still in the national church who could not face the family fights and public ridicule hurled at the dissenters. Seceders continued to suffer social ostracism, economic boycotts, and job blacklists long after the official suppression stopped. Nevertheless, over the next twenty years, the Seceded denomination grew until, by 1869, it boasted one hundred thousand souls and 328 churches served by 232 ministers.[27]

Divisions among Seceders

The seminal years 1834 to 1839, when the Seceder churches grew by leaps and bounds under persecution, were years of relative harmony, but the differing personalities and outlooks of the major leaders made cooperation difficult. Scholte, the leader in the center and south of the country, tried at first to cooperate with de Cock, the leader in the north. This was the "Reformed period" in Scholte's theological life, says his biographer, Lubbertus Oostendorp, before he became enamored with the dispensationalist premillennial views of Bilderdijk and the Englishman, John N. Darby, the founder of the Plymouth Brethren.[28] But already in the first Seceder synod of 1836, fissures were apparent. These came to a head in the 1840s, and the emigrants carried them in their religious baggage to the United States.

Purpose and Goals

Religious reformation is difficult to channel into constructive rather than destructive ways. The Seceder leaders proclaimed independence from the national church, but what did they want to take its place? Some, like de Cock and van Velzen, wanted to restore the Dortian traditions of historic Dutch Calvinism. Others, like Scholte, wanted to restore an experiential gospel

27 J. van Gelderen, "'Scheuring' en Vereniging," in *De Afscheiding van 1834 en haar geschiedenis*, 100-146; Van Dellen, *Secession of 1834*, 32; J.A. de Kok, *Nederland op de breuklijn Rome-Reformatie* (Assen: Van Gorcum, 1964), 292.
28 Oostendorp, *Scholte*, 83.

("primitive Christianity") and congregational independence. Yet a third
way, that of Van Raalte and Brummelkamp, was to adapt the old church
rules to modern times by defending liberty of conscience and building a
church independent from the state. Strong personalities in the center and
extremists and bigots at the fringes plagued the Seceders, as they do every
popular movement.[29]

The Seceders also had their "crisis of youth."[30] A minor matter such as
Scholte's discarding of the old-fashioned clerical cloak caused Budding to
disassociate from him completely. To this van Velzen asked Budding, "Are
you crazy? Or do you want to be the *Pope* completely?" Scholte had to
depose an entire consistory at Stellendam for following a young girl who saw
visions. Every provincial assembly suspended elders and deacons for being
spiritually unfit or holding unorthodox views.[31]

Baptism

The differences among the various Seceders gradually crystallized around
the major issue of the role of the church in society. Was it to establish the
religion of the realm (*Corpus Christianum*—"Body of the Christened") or
to be the religion of true believers (*Corpus Christi*—"Body of Christ")? The
Netherlands Reformed Church clearly was a "realm-religion," but most

29 One of the best analyses is Herbert J. Brinks, "Religious Continuities in Europe
   and the New World," in *The Dutch in America: Immigration, Settlement, and
   Cultural Change*, ed. Robert P. Swierenga (New Brunswick, N.J.: Rutgers
   University Press, 1985), 209-223. Brinks, "Another Look at 1857: The Birth of
   the CRC," *Origins* 4, no. 1 (1986): 27-31, describes the career of another minister
   who shared Scholte's views, the Rev. R.W. Duin, an Ost Frisian Seceder from the
   German Reformed Church who from 1839 to 1841 copastored with van Velzen
   the Seceder churches in Friesland, Groningen, and Drenthe. Duin, with more
   lax German roots, soon became a big problem. He challenged the doctrines of
   election and reprobation as defined in the Canons, approved hymn singing, and
   refused to discipline parishioners who conducted necessary business on Sunday.
   De Cock and van Velzen came to view Duin as a traitor to the Secession and after
   two years of bitter controversy at church assemblies, managed to expel him.
   Brinks argues that the "Duin case" stiffened the spine of the northern wing of the
   Afscheiding for years and shaped the thinking of immigrants in this tradition,
   such as the Drenthers and Graafschapers in Michigan in the 1850s. Dort's
   church rules became the bulwark for preserving the "essentiality of the 1834
   secession" (30).
30 H. Bouwman, *De Crisis der jeugd: Eenige bladzijden uit de geschiedenis van de
   kerken der Afscheiding* (Kampen: J.H. Kok, 1914; reissued 1976).
31 Oostendorp, *Scholte*, 101-103.

Seceders were wary of the heavy hand of the state and leaned toward a "free religion."[32]

The issue, of course, affected views of the sacraments and the church order as well. De Cock followed the standard practice in the national church of baptizing children of baptized but not confessing members, in the belief that God's promises apply to all who attend. This was public christening rather than covenant baptism. Scholte, Brummelkamp, Meerburg, and Budding rejected this "half-way covenant" and insisted that only confessing believers could present their children for the sacrament, since they alone were members of the church of Christ. Van Velzen allowed an elder or other confessing member to present children of baptized members.

Van Raalte originally stood with the Scholte majority on baptism but then wavered, and he eventually followed de Cock's practice. Van Raalte desired the church to be a community church, a *volkskerk*. "Children do not become members of the Congregation by confession of faith, but are members by virtue of the Covenant of Grace.... [Thus] the children of the children of the Congregation must be baptized."[33] He accepted the traditional close ties between the Hervormde Kerk and the Dutch government, including payment of ministers' salaries from the public treasury. Scholte's antithetical view, that of a church free of government funding and control, won out in the synod of 1836, and his position became the policy of the Gereformeerde Kerk in the Netherlands and the Christian Reformed Church in North America. Most Seceders, however, followed de Cock, whose position was adopted at the synod of 1846.[34]

Church Order and Lay Preachers (Oefenaars)

Issues of church governance also threatened to destroy the young Seceder movement. Scholte feared synodical dictates and generally wanted the locus of power to be held in the individual congregation rather than in major assemblies. He proposed a shorter church order, which provincial assemblies adopted in Noord-Brabant, Zuid-Holland, Utrecht, and Lower Gelderland. But Van Velzen, Van Raalte, and de Cock rejected the wholesale revision of

---

32 Leonard Verduin, "CRC: Hewn from the Rock," *The Banner*, 8 October 1984, 9. Verduin further elaborated the distinction in his study booklet, *Honor Your Mother: Christian Reformed Church Roots in the Secession of 1834* (Grand Rapids: CRC Publications, 1988).

33 Free translation from Wormser, *Leven van Albertus Christiaan van Raalte*, 1.

34 Oostendorp, *Scholte*, 103-110, 139-141.

the historic Dortian synodical system and would allow only minor changes. Assemblies in the northern provinces followed Dort. The most debated issue dealt with the status of lay preachers (*oefenaars*), which were allowed by Dort. Scholte wanted them banned, but de Cock believed that the Secession had flourished primarily because of them.[35]

The National Synod of 1837 at Utrecht, under van Velzen's firm hand, hammered out a compromise to try to force unity, which included a ban on lay preachers. The churches of Zeeland agreed, as did Van Raalte in Overijssel, but his Zwolle congregation raised such a storm of protest that Van Raalte "wearied of his life." Zwolle already objected to Van Raalte's giving up the minister's coat, and now he rejected lay preachers. Several of Van Raalte's congregations, including Zwolle, Zalk, and Mastenbroek, joined the Reformed Churches under the Cross, which met in the conventicle style with elders reading sermons of the "old writers." A leader in the breakaway group against Van Raalte was Rev. Douwe J. Vander Werp (1811-1876), a student of de Cock who after 1864 became a leader in the Christian Reformed Church in America. Van Velzen blamed his old school friend Scholte for the new secession, and the church order debate became a personal quarrel. Van Raalte defended Scholte at first but not for long.[36]

Scholte deposed—1840

The quarrel between van Velzen and Scholte escalated into a splintering among the Seceders that led to Scholte's deposition from office in 1840. Amsterdam was the battleground. The break began in 1839 when the Amsterdam congregation, which Scholte had formed in 1835, in a close vote called van Velzen over Scholte to be its pastor. Van Velzen accepted the call but strangely did not leave his post in Friesland to take up the work in

35 Oostendorp, *Scholte*, 112-115. The complete acts of the general synods of the Christian Seceder Reformed Church are published in *Handelingen en verslagen van de algemene synoden van de Christelijk Afgescheidene Gereformeerde Kerk (1836-1869)* (Houten/Utrecht: Den Hartog, 1984).

36 Since the so-called "Kruiskerken" had no ordained pastors, elders installed each other to office. Elder Vander Werp, for example, was ordained by elder A. Schouwenberg, and then Vander Werp ordained Schouwenberg. Oostendorp, *Scholte*, 115-116 (quote 115), citing *Officieele Stukken uit het Nederlandsch Herv. Kerkgenootschap* (Kampen, 1863), which are the official minutes of the various synods. In 1841, Ledeboer led another secession of churches who followed his experiential style. The Ledeboerian churches, however, remained independent and never formed a denomination.

Simon van Velzen as Kampen Professor

Hendrik P. Scholte, 1862

Amsterdam. In the face of this irregular "acceptance," Scholte began holding separate services in Amsterdam. Scholte's Utrecht consistory then charged that van Velzen's preaching overemphasized divine election and was coldly formal. He "preached a conglomeration of theoretical truths without the living Christ, without a regenerating Spirit, and without the living and active faith." To this, van Velzen cried "Slander!"[37]

At its heart, the dispute centered around subtle historic differences regarding the doctrine of election and human responsibility that stirred the Reformed churches since the Synod of Dort. Van Velzen and his supporters stressed human depravity and inability. As van Velzen thundered in a sermon: "Man *can do nothing*, yea, *may not* do anything" to attain salvation, "because this would be one's own work, and that such work is condemned before God." Scholte and the others agreed on the need for divine grace, but they would not so denigrate the human condition. This raised the ghost of Arminius for van Velzen.[38]

The upshot was that the Synod of 1840, meeting at Amsterdam, did not investigate van Velzen's theology but demanded that Scholte retract his

37 Oostendorp, *Scholte*, 118-128 (quote 122).
38 Oostendorp, *Scholte*, 123; Brinks, "De Afscheiding," 26.

Western Seminary Collection,
Joint Archives of Holland

Carel G. de Moen

*Anthony Brummelkamp as Kampen
Professor*

"slander" of the brother and unconditionally accept the 1619 Dort church order. When Scholte refused, the synod suspended him from the ministry. Thus, as Oostendorp says, did the young Seceder denomination lose one of its "most capable leaders." The major voting block against Scholte was the four brothers-in-law—van Velzen, Brummelkamp, Van Raalte, and Carel G. de Moen (1811-1879), plus de Cock. The synod also gave up all attempts at revising church polity and adopted almost verbatim the historic church order.[39]

After Scholte's deposition, many churches in Utrecht, Zuid-Holland, and Zeeland continued to recognize him as a brother, and Van Raalte also tried to rehabilitate him. When the next synod assembled in 1843, again in Amsterdam, Scholte actually appeared, and the delegates worshiped together and tried to effect a reconciliation. Van Raalte offered a resolution asking everyone to accept the Dort order as "binding." He and van Velzen voted "yes," but Scholte and Brummelkamp said "no." Van Raalte and twenty-one

---

39 Oostendorp, *Scholte*, 126. No churches from Zeeland, Noord-Brabant, Zuid-Holland, or Utrecht participated in the 1840 Synod.

other delegates then left the meeting, and the gathering adjourned.[40] After this, Scholte adopted the premillennial ideas of Bilderdijk, da Costa, and Darby, and all possibility of reconciliation ended.

Southern "center" party, Northern "right" party, and Scholte "left" party

Although the Secession of 1834 was a series of locally oriented reformations, rather than a centrally organized movement, the various factions soon coalesced into larger groupings, which can truly be called "brother's quarrels" (*broedertwisten*), because Van Raalte and Brummelkamp ended up on one side and van Velzen on the other. In the center of the religious spectrum was an urban and liberal southern party, led by Brummelkamp, Van Raalte, Scholte (in the early years), and Vander Meulen, which was concentrated in the provinces of Overijssel and Gelderland, with lesser contingents in Noord- and Zuid-Holland, Utrecht, Noord-Brabant, Zeeland, and Ost Friesland. On the right stood the rural and very orthodox northern party led by de Cock and van Velzen, which was concentrated in the provinces of Groningen, Friesland, and Drenthe, with related groups of conservative Zeelanders led by Budding and many Graafschapers.[41]

Scholte increasingly after 1840 moved to the extreme left, espousing a separatist, pietist, premillennial, nonconfessional Christianity—"no creed but the Bible." He became the lone ranger, going into nontraditional paths that led to "ecclesiastical anarchy"—to use Van Raalte's words—where few other leaders would follow.[42]

The northern party defended the doctrine, liturgy, and polity of Dort as biblically grounded; they were strongly traditional Calvinists who stressed

40 Oostendorp, *Scholte*, 128-131.
41 Henry Beets, *De Chr. Geref. Kerk in N.A.: Zestig Jaren van Strijd en Zegen* (Grand Rapids: Grand Rapids Printing Co., 1918), 34-36, 45-48. Beets distinguishes the de Cock-Joffers-van Velzen alliance as the northern party, and the Brummelkamp-Scholte alliance as the southern Geldersche party. The factions were also called van Velzianen and Brummelkampianen. Cf. John Kromminga, *The Christian Reformed Church: A Study in Orthodoxy* (Grand Rapids: Baker Book House, 1949), 30-31. An English translation of Beets' denominational history is available in the Calvin College Archives, Grand Rapids, Mich.
42 *Classis Holland Minutes 1848-1858*, 221. William O. Van Eyck, *Landmarks of the Reformed Fathers, Or What Dr. Van Raalte's People Believed* (Grand Rapids: Reformed Press, 1922), 140, picks up on this phrase too. Scholte deserves to be studied anew, since his way of nondenominational congregationalism and biblicism has become dominant in American evangelicalism. On this point see Earl William Kennedy, "Eden in the Heartland," *The Church Herald* 54 (March 1997): 8-10, 15.

the need for Christian schools and catechetical instruction of the youth, given the "Godless influence" in the public schools. The northern faction had steel in their bones, while the southern party had rubber. The southern party was more broad-minded, inclusive, and even-tempered; it stressed experiential piety and evangelism to the point that some charged them with Arminian leanings. They did not glory in the Secession but rather longed to return to the national church, provided that its leaders were willing to seek Bible-based reformation. In 1842 Van Raalte and C.G. de Moen took the remarkable step of publishing an "Appeal" to the General Synod of the Hervormde Kerk on behalf of the Seceded churches in Ommen and Den Ham, which called for "a true linking of all upright reformed people, separated as well as not separated Christians.... We still feel connected to those in the Church who forever love Christ," the brothers-in-law confessed in the document that ended with their personal signatures.[43]

The Afscheiding factions presaged divisions that would occur later in America, which were merely a continuation of old battles, with a new issue thrown in, that of Americanization. As Herbert Brinks explained cogently, "Though the general lines of descent display astounding complexities, it is clear that the Christian Reformed Church and its Protestant Reformed offshoot originated from de Cock's adherents while the Reformed Church in America attracted Van Raalte and his disciples.[44]

Among the Seceders who emigrated in the crucial 1840s when entire congregations left for America, the southern element was stronger than in later years when the northern contingent predominated. For example, 93 percent of all Seceder emigrants from the province of Utrecht between 1844 and 1880 departed before 1857. Comparable figures for other southern provinces in these early years are Gelderland, 71 percent; Zuid-Holland, 80 percent; and Noord-Brabant, 72 percent. In the northern province of Groningen, on the other hand, the rate of Seceder emigration increased

---

43 A.C. Van Raalte and C.G. de Moen, *Adres aan de Algemene Synode van het Nederlandsch Hervormd Kerkgenootschap* (Ommen: E. ten Tooren, 1842). A copy is in the Calvin College Archives. An English translation by Simone Kennedy is available at the A. C. Van Raalte Institute.

44 Herbert J. Brinks, "De Afscheiding: 1834-1984," *Origins* 2, no. 2 (1984): 26. Brinks adds that Scholte's independent, millennial tradition was evident in the Rev. Harry Bultema and his followers in 1918, and the "Cross Churches" and Ledeboerians find their children in the Netherlands Reformed Church in America.

over the years, from 20 percent in the early period to 32 percent from 1858 through 1868, and 48 percent from 1869 through 1880. It was the large influx of Groningen farm laborers after the Civil War that spurred the growth of the Christian Reformed Church in those years.

Conclusion

The Secession of 1834 was a reformation in the Hervormde Kerk that started small but had a far-reaching impact in the Netherlands and across the seas in North America, South Africa, and elsewhere. The central issue was a return to Dordrecht, to the doctrinal integrity, church governance, and practices of the seventeenth century. The controversy risked tearing the church apart in sectarian struggles and personality conflicts. The descendants of these leaders can be thankful that they overcame the difficulties, saved the reformation, and even planted a renewed church here in a new environment. The Dutch Reformed churches in America are truly daughters of the Secession of 1834. We cannot understand ourselves without knowing our mother, the Christian Seceded Church of the Netherlands.

II
1850

The Union of 1850:
The Classis of Holland Joins
the Reformed Protestant
Dutch Church

The Reformed believers of the Holland, Michigan, area celebrated two significant sesquicentennial events in 1997 and 1998—the founding of the Holland colony (1847) and the organizing of the Classis of Holland (1848), which is the parent ecclesiastical organization of the midwestern churches of the Reformed Church in America. In the year 2000, they anticipate another 150th anniversary—the Union of 1850 of the Classis of Holland with the RCA. The union was significant for the RCA because without it the frontier mission efforts of the denomination would not have flourished, and in the long term, the process of Americanization would have been greatly accelerated. This aspect is detailed in the conclusion of this chapter. For the Christian Reformed Church the Union decision was its raison d'etre. It was the objection to this union that led directly to the Secession of 1857.

The Union of 1850 engendered so much intense discussion in the succeeding years that it is difficult to achieve a balanced view of what actually led to it. The CRC and RCA historiography is such that if the writer is CRC, the Union of 1850 was bad and the Secession of 1857 was good. The reverse is true for the RCA. For pro-union RCA scholars, consult William O. Van Eyck who is the most biased of the RCA writers; Aleida Pieters, the daughter of the second pastor of Pillar Church; and Gerhard De Jonge.[1] Interestingly enough, Jacob van Hinte, a Dutch sociologist who wrote the monumental work on Netherlanders in America, favored the RCA point of view.[2] Anti-union CRC writers are Henry Beets, Diedrich Kromminga, and Albert Hyma.[3] I will try to achieve the goal set by the late president of Calvin Theological Seminary, John H. Kromminga, who is a model for the religious historian on the topic of the Union of 1850 and the Secession of 1857.[4] Dick L. Van Halsema, former president of the Reformed Bible College, was also very balanced in his understanding of the Union of 1850, although both he and Kromminga had valid questions about it.[5]

Another Look at the Netherlands Hervormde Kerk

An understanding of the subject of the Union of 1850 must begin by asking a theological question: what constitutes a true church? The answer to this theological question governs the conclusions one makes about the Secession of 1834 and the Union of 1850.

Rev. Hendrik de Cock wrote a pamphlet when he led the secession from the Hervormde Kerk in 1834 entitled, "Act of Secession and Return."[6] The

---

[1]   The works of these authors are, respectively: William O. Van Eyck, *The Union of 1850, A Collection of Papers by the Late Wm. O. Van Eyck, Esq. On the Union of the Classis of Holland With the Reformed Church in America, In June, 1850* (Grand Rapids: Wm. B. Eerdmans, 1950); Aleida Peters, *A Dutch Settlement in Michigan* (Grand Rapids: Eerdmans-Sevensma, 1923); and Gerhard De Jonge, "The Union of the Classis of Holland with the Reformed Church in America," Gerhard De Jonge Papers, Western Seminary Collection, Joint Archives of Holland, Holland, Mich..

[2]   Jacob van Hinte, *Netherlanders in America: A Study of Emigration and Settlement in the Nineteenth and Twentieth Centuries in the United States of America* (1928), ed. Robert P. Swierenga, trans. Adriaan de Wit (Grand Rapids: Baker Book House, 1985).

[3]   Henry Beets, *The Christian Reformed Church: Its Roots, History, Schools and Mission Work, A.D. 1857 to 1946* (Grand Rapids: Baker Book House, 1946); Diedrich Kromminga, *The Christian Reformed Tradition: From the Reformation Till the Present* (Grand Rapids: Wm. B. Eerdmans, 1943); and Albert Hyma, *Albertus C. Van Raalte and His Dutch Settlements in the United States* (Grand Rapids: Wm. B. Eerdmans, 1947).

[4]   John H. Kromminga, *The Christian Reformed Church: A Study in Orthodoxy* (Grand Rapids: Baker Book House, 1949).

[5]   Dick L. Van Halsema's valuable essay on the Secession of 1822 is entitled, "Hopkins, Hackensack, and Haan," *Reformed Journal*, January 1957, 7-9.

key thrust of the document was that the Hervormde Kerk had become a false church and showed few, if any, marks of the true church. The issue, then, is how one decides whether a church or denomination is false or true in light of the three traditional Calvinistic criteria of the church: (1) Is the Word rightly preached? (2) Are the sacraments rightly administered? and (3) Is discipline properly exercised?

De Cock's defenders have always claimed that he was correct in calling the Hervormde Kerk a false church. But in light of John Calvin's criteria, it was not a false church but one in transition. The best excuse for secession at any time is the declaration that the parent organization is false. This is what the churches of the Hackensack Classis did in 1822 when they declared that the RCA was a false church and produced the Secession of 1822. It is also a contemporary issue for the CRC.[7] Since approximately one-tenth of the membership of the CRC has left the denomination in recent years, it is relevant to ask how the CRC is pictured by the seceding members who have formed independent congregations that protest the ordination of women and other decisions? Are some former CRC members now calling the CRC a false church, untrue to Scripture? The question of whether a church is false, rather than declining or changing, is a timely one. With that question in mind, it is necessary to review briefly the 200-year history of the Hervormde Kerk (or *Gereformeerde Kerk* as it was known until 1816), from the bedrock of the Synod of Dort, 1618-1619.[8]

As Gerrit ten Zythoff said, "There [in the synod], the orthodox scholastic party led by [Franciscus] Gomarus was victorious over the biblical-humanistic wing of [Jacobus] Arminius's followers.[9]" When we hear the name Arminius,

---

6   Gerrit tenZythoff, *Sources of Secession: The Netherlands Hervormde Kerk on the Eve of the Dutch Immigration to the Midwest* (Grand Rapids: Wm. B. Eerdmans, 1987); Van Hinte, *Netherlanders in America,* 88-96.

7   Darrell Todd Maurina, "CRC numbers drop to '71 levels," *Holland Sentinel,* 23 February 1997, Al-A2. A quote from the article reads as follows: "The CRC's most recent yearbook reports that the denomination lost 5,932 members, or just over 2 percent of its membership in 1996, falling to a total of 285,864. That brought to 30,551 the number of church members it's lost over the past five years, with many of the departing members believed to have joined a growing conservative secession movement."

8   For a brief review of this history, see Elton J. Bruins, "From Calvin to Van Raalte: The Rise and Development of the Reformed Tradition in the Netherlands, 1560-1900," in *Servant Gladly: Essays in Honor of John W. Beardslee III,* ed. Jack D. Klunder and Russell L. Gasero (Grand Rapids: Wm. B. Eerdmans, 1989).

9   TenZythoff, *Sources of Secession,* 10.

Jacobus Arminius   *Franciscus Gomarus*

we easily equate it with the term free will. But we need to understand that when Arminius used the term free will, he was using it within the context of moderate Calvinism and not what came to be known as Arminianism which the Methodists came to espouse or what Baptists like Billy Graham hold today. Billy Graham once said, "If you will, you can be saved." That's Arminianism. What Arminius himself claimed is the basic Calvinistic position of seeing how the will functions when a person is making a response to God by grace. Arminius, a moderate Calvinist in comparison with his teacher, Theodore Beza, wanted to avoid anything that looked like determinism, so he rejected the supralapsarian or ultra Calvinistic position of some delegates at the synod, such as Gomarus, Arminius's opponent.

Following the Synod of Dort, two major trends of theological thinking developed, one led by Johannes Coccejus, the theologian at Leiden, and the other led by Gisbertus Voetius of Utrecht. Even though the synod played such a decisive role in the history of the Hervormde Kerk, there nevertheless developed different points of view during the next two centuries. The views of Voetius are the most important, because he and his followers in the Secession of 1834 played a crucial role in the church life of the Netherlands. Voetius was a strong proponent of true piety in believers, as well as careful Sabbath observance. Anyone who has grown up in a Reformed Christian

Gisbertus Voetius

community and was not allowed to ride a bicycle on Sunday was likely a beneficiary of Voetian influence!

According to Gerrit ten Zythoff, "Dordtian orthodoxy lost its uniformity in the bifurcation of a right and left wing" in the Netherlands Hervormde Kerk.[10] Jean de Labadie and his followers stood on the extreme right of the spectrum. On the left stood Hofstede de Groot and other ministers and leaders, who were influenced by the Enlightenment liberalism of Friedrich E. D. Schleiermacher, the German theologian. Men like Albertus C. Van Raalte's father were probably in the middle of the spectrum.[11] De Cock after his conversion moved from the left of the spectrum to a position quite far to the right. In short, there was a great diversity of thinking in the Hervormde Kerk.

Moreover, when the Hervormde Kerk lost its privileged position under Napoleon in 1795, many serious Christians became very troubled. The

---

[10] Ibid., 11.
[11] Gerald De Jong, *The Dutch Reformed Church in the American Colonies* (Grand Rapids: Wm. B. Eerdmans, 1978), 44-46; tenZythoff, *Sources of Secession*, 104-110, 118-120.

intellectual elite were no longer Calvinistic but believers in natural religion, who founded a belief in God on reason and not revelation.[12] The Hervormde Kerk in the early nineteenth century lost its hegemony and influence, but it still contained many true Christians, such as the Van Raalte family. Therefore, de Cock was incorrect in calling the Hervormde Kerk false; it was a church undergoing great change and perhaps even declension, but was not apostate. However, de Cock may have rightfully challenged believers in that church to come out and be separate, because he felt as a leader he could no longer exercise his ministry in that church.

Van Raalte's views were colored by the fact that his father spent his entire career as a pastor in the Hervormde Kerk. Van Raalte also intended to enter the ministry of that church when he graduated from Leiden in 1835, the year *after* the secession had begun. He did not do so because, *after* raising reservations about some of the church's regulations, church authorities would not approve his candidacy unless he recanted. Consequently, he was rejected for ministry in the Hervormde Kerk.

Lest we think that Van Raalte was a reluctant secessionist, he was not.[13] During his ten years of ministry in the church of the Afgescheidenen (1836-1846), he and his wife Christina fought valiantly for the cause. He served the Separatist congregations of Genemuiden, Mastenbroek, Ommen, and Arnhem, and paid a large amount in fines for his preaching. Van Raalte was jailed once for twelve days. He was a pioneer in developing the program of theological education for training young men for ministry in the Christian Seceded Church. Van Raalte was considered a troublemaker by the Dutch authorities. There can be no doubt about his credentials when it came to his service in the Afscheiding.

But the key theological question remains the nature of the church. Van Raalte, whose mother, sisters, and brothers remained in the Hervormde Kerk, along with the leaders of the *Réveil* and many other pious people,

---

[12] Ibid., 27-28.

[13] H. Reenders gives a full account of Van Raalte's ministry in Overijssel Province, 1836-1846, in his essay, "Albertus C. van Raalte als leider van Overijsselse Afgescheidenen," in *"Van scheurmakers, onruststokers en geheime opruijers..."* *De Afscheiding in Overijssel* (Kampen: Uitgave Ijsselakademie, 1984), 98-197. On the other hand, Reenders noted that Van Raalte was the most ecumenical in spirit of all the secessionist leaders. See Reenders essay, "Albertus C. van Raalte: The *Homo Oecumenicus* among the Secession Leaders," *Calvin Theological Journal* 33, no. 2 (1998), 277-298

Theological School, Ommen

Gereformeerde Kerk, Ommen

never considered the Hervormde Kerk as a false church but one in danger of moving toward apostasy. Many dedicated Christians in the Hervormde Kerk knew that the church was in decline but chose to remain in the church and work for its betterment rather than to leave it.

Hear Van Raalte in his own words: "As for me, I hated it to be able no longer to occupy the pulpits of my father, to become a shame to my relatives and to my mother during her lifetime; for me it was the most painful sacrifice to give up the so fervently desired preaching from the country's pulpits."[14] At heart, I believe that Van Raalte considered the Hervormde Kerk a church in decline but not an apostate church. For similar reasons, he was very open to union with the Reformed Dutch Church in America, a child of the Gereformeerde (later Hervormde) Kerk in the Netherlands, after he examined the theology and piety of that church.

The Reformed Dutch Church of North America, 1628-1850

When Van Raalte and his followers came to America, beginning in late 1846, they met representatives of the RCA, which resulted in a union with the old Dutch church three and one-half years later. Several matters need to be examined in order to understand why he moved so quickly to unite with this body in America. This question is crucial because it has been raised

[14] TenZythoff, *Sources of Secession*, 29.

repeatedly, especially by those who went into the CRC. Therefore, a brief review of the history of the RCA is necessary in order to get a perspective on the question.[15]

The Reformed Church in America takes 1628 as its founding date, a date only nine years after the conclusion of the great Synod of Dort. The Dutch West India Company, wishing to do business in the New World, set up a colony for trade on Manhattan Island in the early 1620s. The company also brought in comforters of the sick and pastors to minister to the colonists in New Netherland.

Thus, the Reformed Protestant Dutch Church, as the denomination was known for many years, got a toehold in New Amsterdam, which remained a Dutch colony until 1664 when the English conquered the settlement and changed the name to New York. The Dutch church grew slowly but surely and began to spread east into areas which are now the Brooklyn and Queens sections of New York City, north up the Hudson River to Albany, and west into New Jersey. The members of the Dutch church held on to their native language for worship even though English became the dominant language in the American colonies. The church developed enough strength that when it declared independence from the Gereformeerde Kerk in the Netherlands in 1792, it was even a majority church in America along with the Congregationalists, Methodists, Baptists, and Presbyterians. Theodorus Frelinghuysen, a pastor trained in the Voetian tradition, who had come from the Netherlands about 1720 to serve the Raritan, New Jersey, congregation, had great success in New Jersey. He was a leader in the First Great Awakening, followed by William and Gilbert Tennant who were Presbyterians, and Jonathan Edwards, the great Congregationalist pastor, theologian, and revivalist.[16]

So on the one hand the Dutch church had its successes. It also had its failures, however. It was rent by a serious division in the mid-eighteenth century over the issue of ordination. The question was whether ministerial candidates had to be educated and ordained in the Netherlands or whether they could be trained and ordained in America. Today it is very difficult to

---

[15] There is no complete scholarly history of the Reformed Church in America. However, Gerald De Jong covers the first two centuries in his definitive work, *Dutch Reformed Church in the American Colonies*. A popular history is Arie R. Brouwer's *Reformed Church Roots, Thirty-Five Formative Events* (New York: Reformed Church Press, 1977).

[16] De Jong, *Dutch Reformed Church,* 173-178.

John H. Livingston

imagine that the pro-Dutch party in the church, called Conferentie, insisted that every candidate had to sail back to the Netherlands for ordination, following the orders of the Classis of Amsterdam to which the Dutch churches in the new world were accountable.

The pro-American party, which went by the name Coetus (pronounced "seetus"), urged strongly that the American Dutch church be allowed to train its ministers and have the right to ordain them. The Classis of Amsterdam insisted generally that the candidates be examined in the Netherlands to ensure the maintenance of ministerial standards. The American Dutch church divided. The Conferentie candidates went back to the Netherlands for ordination and the Coetus party trained and ordained candidates contrary to regulations of the Netherlands Reformed Church. The deeper issue was the pace of Americanization for the Dutch congregations in the American colonies.

The matter was not settled until 1771, when John H. Livingston, a Yale graduate who took his theological education at Utrecht and stood in the Voetian tradition, organized the Union Convention and brought together the opposing parties. Peace in the church was restored. The Coetus party had founded Queen's College in 1766, later called Rutgers College, for the training of ministers. But the Revolutionary War came in 1776 and convulsed the country until 1783. Many Dutch churches were damaged or destroyed by the British. Livingston became the pastor of the Dutch Church in New York and also established theological education on American soil for the Dutch churches, which resulted in the founding of the New Brunswick Theological Seminary in 1784, a year after the war ended.[17]

Livingston also organized the RCA into an American denomination in 1792. During and after the war, all major contact with the Netherlands came to an end. The Classis of Amsterdam no longer had jurisdiction over its American branch. The daughter church became an adult, proceeding on her own. Livingston, a key leader, was pastor of the most prominent congregation of the RCA, the Collegiate Church of New York. He came out of the patrician Livingston family, which was not Dutch but English in lineage. He had a superior education at Yale and Utrecht. There was no question about his sterling credentials or training, as well as his native ability and skills.

In 1792, the constitution Livingston prepared, which adapted the Dutch liturgy for America, was approved by the Reformed Dutch Church in America, a transplant of the Hervormde Kerk. The denomination followed the church in the Netherlands in the three forms of unity: the Heidelberg Catechism, the Belgic Confession, and the Canons of the Synod of Dort. One change Livingston made, however, was to adapt the Dort church order to the American scene.[18]

Most significant was the fact that the Reformed Dutch Church in America did not experience to any extent the influences of the Enlightenment and its liberalizing tendencies as did the mother church in the Netherlands. Of course, the American church did not have to deal with the matter of disestablishment as did the Netherlands church. That matter had already been dealt with in 1664 when England conquered New Netherland. Likewise, America was not overrun by Napoleon and the French army. In short, the RCA remained basically orthodox while the mother church in the Netherlands became liberal, which led many of the Afscheiding ministers to claim that the mother church had become false.

---

17 Ibid., 188-210.
18 The full text of the Explanatory Articles is found in *A Digest of Constitutional and Synodical Legislation of the Reformed Church in America [Formerly the Ref. Prot. Dutch Church]* by Edward T. Corwin (New York: Board of Publication of the Reformed Church in America, 1906), v-lxxxvii.

The RCA, nevertheless, underwent a painful and difficult secession in 1822. Some ministers under the leadership of the Rev. Solomon Froeligh claimed that the RCA had moderated its Dortian Calvinism by becoming Hopkinsian, which is to say, that it followed the departure from standard Reformed doctrine espoused by the New England theologian, Samuel Hopkins. For one thing, Hopkins denied original sin.[19] Therefore, Froeligh and his cohorts claimed that the RCA had lost its moorings.[20] These ministers then established a new denomination that they called the "True Reformed Dutch Church," which implied (as de Cock claimed in 1834) that the mother church was the false church and all true believers must depart her realms.

The General Synod of the RCA in 1824 responded to the so-called True Reformed Dutch Church by rejecting the charge of Hopkinsianism and vigorously reaffirming its historic confessions. A section of the General Synod minutes of 1824 read:

> Resolved, That while this Synod totally disapprove of the late secession, and of all the means that have been employed to promote it, they do decidedly disown and condemn any such doctrines . . . set forth in such publications, and the doctrines commonly called Hopkinsian, as being contrary to the work of God, and the standards of the Reformed Dutch Church, and at the same time as decidedly condemn the course pursued by ministers and members of the late secession, who by *their* publications and conversation, and other measures, have endeavoured to establish the belief that such are the views of the Reformed Dutch Church, which views this Synod unequivocally pronounce altogether calumnious.[21]

[19] Daniel G. Reid, ed. *Dictionary of Christianity in America* (Downers Grove, Ill.: InterVarsity Press, 1990), 553-554. Beets in *Christian Reformed Church* uncritically accepted the reasoning of the 1822 seceders, while Dick L. Van Halsema demolished their arguments in "Hopkins, Hackensack, and Haan," *Reformed Journal*, January 1957, 79. Van Halsema said: "From the viewpoint of historical accuracy, it can be seen that Froeligh and his fellows may have made a mountain out of a mole-hill." The conclusion of this article was that Froeligh and his sympathizers were mainly malcontents and did not have a valid reason for seceding from the RCA.

[20] A good but brief biographical sketch of Solomon Froeligh and the role he played in the Secession of 1822 is William C. Kiessel, Jr., "Solomon Froeligh, D.D." *Reformed Journal*, July-August 1954, 11-13.

[21] *The Acts and Proceedings of the General Synod of the Reformed Dutch Church in North America, at New-York, June, 1824,* 52.

The congregations that left the RCA in 1822 formed the Classis of Hackensack and united with the CRC in the latter part of the nineteenth century.

The effects of the secession of 1822 were as damaging to the RCA as the Coetus-Conferentie controversy in the previous century had been. There was the loss of members and congregations. The disaffection came at a bad time for the RCA. The Methodist and Baptists were growing rapidly and moving west with the pioneers. The RCA had been a majority church, but it now lost that status to other denominations, including the Presbyterians.

The character of the RCA in 1846, the year Van Raalte and his followers arrived in America, can be summarized as conservative, orthodox, and Americanized. After all, the RCA was more than 200 years old in 1846. The language of the church was English, although a few people could still speak Dutch, such as Revs. Thomas De Witt and Isaac Wyckoff, whom Van Raalte came to know well after he arrived in New York. People from many backgrounds had entered the RCA, including Germans of Reformed persuasion from the Palatine in the Rhineland who had settled in New York state, and French Huguenots who settled in places like New Paltz, New York. Overall, the denomination was distinctly different from the Hervormde Kerk, and yet it was similar in faith and practice with all faithful members of the Hervormde and Gereformeerde churches.

The Welcome of the RCA to Van Raalte and his Followers

When Van Raalte and his parishioners decided to emigrate in the summer of 1846, they knew very little about America or the RCA. Some people who had emigrated the year before sent letters to him, such as Roelof Sleijster of Alto, Wisconsin, one of his former theological students. Alexander Hartgerink, his parishioner from Velp, had also gone to America and wrote favorably about his new homeland. Overall, Van Raalte was basically naive about the United States. However, he felt God was leading him and his people to a new place of settlement in America, but like Abraham, he did not know where he was going.

Providentially, a distinguished leader in the American church was sent to the Netherlands by the RCA during the spring of 1846 to search for documents of the Classis of Amsterdam relating to its history. That person was Rev. Dr. Thomas De Witt, pastor of the Collegiate Dutch Church in New York City. When De Witt visited the Netherlands he became acquainted with the Afscheiding movement by meeting with Rev. Hendrik P. Scholte.

Archives of the Reformed Church in America

Thomas De Witt

Through Scholte, De Witt had his introduction to the Christian Seceded Church and was very impressed with its piety and seriousness of purpose. Upon his return De Witt wrote:

> During my recent short visit to Holland, I became partially acquainted with this movement [that is, the secession from the old Established Reformed Church who strictly adhere to the faith of their fathers], and found it commanded deep interest, and that large numbers are ready to enlist in it. Very many of them are of the class who are struggling by honest industry to obtain a mere living, and stand in need of aid to take the preparatory steps to leave their own country and make their settlement in America. A few individuals of their number some time since, settled in our Western States, and have written to them in language of encouragement and promise. [22]

For some reason, De Witt did not meet Van Raalte in the Netherlands. The two first met upon Van Raalte's arrival on the docks in New York.

[22] Henry S. Lucas, *Dutch Immigrant Memoirs and Related Writings*, 2 vols. (Assen, the Netherlands: von Gorcum, 1955; reprint, Grand Rapids: Wm B. Eerdmans, 1997), 1:24. The quote comes from a news item which appeared in the *Christian Intelligencer*, 8 October 1846.

Isaac N. Wyckoff

After returning to New York, De Witt immediately began to use the columns of the *Christian Intelligencer*, the weekly periodical of the RCA, to inform readers about the expected Dutch immigrants. In the issue of 8 October 1846, he reported that a "Protestant Evangelical Holland Emigrant Society" had been founded in Albany by Isaac N. Wyckoff, pastor of the Second Reformed Church, to assist the immigrants passing through that city. De Witt wrote often of Van Raalte, Scholte, and their plans to emigrate. Just a week later, De Witt published a translation of a tract of Antonie Brummelkamp and Van Raalte, named "Appeal to the Faithful in America," which had been published five months earlier (25 May 1846) in the Netherlands.

On 3 December De Witt notified readers that Van Raalte had arrived in New York and left for Wisconsin. More news items appeared in succeeding issues.[23] The 4 February 1847 issue reported that De Witt had established another society to assist immigrants, "The Netherlands Society for the Protection of Emigrants from Holland," and it pleaded for funds to assist the destitute Hollanders[24]. In the next months (11 February, 11, 17, 25 March,

23 *Christian Intelligencer*, 31 December 1846; 7 January and 4 February 1847.
24 Van Hinte, *Netherlanders in America*, 303.

6, 13 May) all kinds of plans and pleas for help were placed before RCA readers in the *Christian Intelligencer*. This made them very aware of Van Raalte and his people as they made their way West.

Isaac Wyckoff became the best known person to the majority of the Holland colony people, because the Board of Domestic Missions of the RCA sent him to the colony in June 1849 to review their needs. The colonists welcomed him gladly, since they remembered how much he and his society had done for them on their travels through New York. Wyckoff was in the Holland colony for nearly a week. Upon his return, he wrote a report to the Board of Domestic Missions, which is probably the most crucial document for understanding the Union of 1850.

In his report, Wyckoff said, "My reception, as your messenger, by the Colony was met almost literally with a shout of joy."[25] But he also added immediately, "There had been sorrow in the colony over many things and not least over the fact that the Dutch Church [which they had hoped would have reached the poor emigrants, flying in poverty from persecution, with sympathizing hearts and open arms] had seemed to take almost no interest at all in them. With the exception of a few individual brethren, they mourned that the Dutch Church counted them strangers, and had no word of encouragement, no hand of help for them. The reaction, therefore, was electrical. To think that we at last felt for them [cared for them, were willing to help them though late] shot through every heart, and there were many thanksgivings to God for His work of love, and many benedictions on the head of your representative." Even though De Witt and Wyckoff and their societies provided significant aid to the immigrants, the colonists had expected much more!

Wyckoff reported that five of the seven congregations in the classis had erected houses of worship. Zeeland's was really better built and nicer looking than Holland's, he observed, but at least these congregations had roofs over their heads when they gathered for worship. Van Raalte was serving this congregation, Cornelius Vander Meulen was at Zeeland, Marten Ypma in Vriesland, and Seine Bolks in Overisel. Hendrik G. Klijn (Kleijn or Klyn) was on his way to America to serve the Graafschap congregation.

---

[25] Lucas published the full report of Wyckoff in *Dutch Immigrant Memoirs and Related Writings*, 1:448-457.

Cornelius Vander Meulen

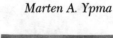

Marten A. Ypma

Hendrik G. Klijn

Seine Bolks

A key section of the report was Wyckoff's invitation to the classis to unite with the RCA. This part of his report entered significally into the discussion concerning the Secession of 1857. He wrote:

> At the classical meeting it was soon made known that the brethren were a little afraid of entering into ecclesiastical connection with us although they believe in the union of brethren and sigh for Christian sympathy and association. They have so felt the galling chains of ecclesiastical domination and have seen with sorrow how exact organization according to human rules leads to formality on the one hand and to the oppression of tender consciences on the

Holland Museum Collection,
Joint Archives of Holland

Settlers' Log Church

Hope College Collection,
Joint Archives of Holland

Albertus C. Van Raalte

other that they hardly know what to say. I protested, of course, that it was the farthest from our thoughts to bring them in bondage to men or to exercise an ecclesiastical tyranny over them. And I stated that they would be most perfectly free at any time they found an ecclesiastical connection opposed to their religious prosperity or enjoyment to bid us a fraternal adieu and be by themselves again.[26]

Wyckoff's visit to the colony was the first contact of the RCA with the Classis of Holland. But communication had been established at least eight months earlier according to article eight of the minutes of the second meeting of the classis, 27 September 1848: "By Rev. Vander Meulen the assembly is informed that an invitation has been received from the Dutch Church, or the old Holland churches, to attend their Synodical assemblies.

[26] Ibid., 1:454.

Zeeland First Log Church

Western Seminary Collection,
Joint Archives of Holland

Graafschap Log Church

However, although it is acknowledged that we should seek greater intercourse with one another, and that it is a requirement of love to exercise fellowship; nevertheless, at this moment it is difficult to do so, because of the pressure of local business and the difficulties connected with a new settlement."[27]

There is no mention of the RCA in the next classis meeting on 25 April 1849, which took place just a month before Wyckoff's visit. There may well have been some mention of the RCA at the meeting, but the clerk of the classis died suddenly after that meeting and the formal minutes were never written up fully, only summarized later. However, very soon after the Wyckoff visit, twenty-four ministers and elders of the classis published a

[27] *Classis Holland Minutes 1848-1858* (Grand Rapids: Wm. B. Eerdmans, 1950), 26-27.

report, written most likely by Van Raalte and dated 10 July, entitled: "Substance of what was transacted at a meeting of the ministers and some of the elders of the churches in the Holland Colony, held June 1849 at Holland, Ottawa Co., Michigan, *in response to certain questions for information proposed by Dr. Wyckoff, of Albany, N. Y., thereunto duly commissioned by the Board of Domestic Missions.*"[28]

Of the twenty-four people who signed this key document, four were ministers: Van Raalte, Vander Meulen, Ypma, and Bolks. Of the sixteen elders only eight attended the April classis meeting.[29] Of those eight, five were from the Zeeland congregation and three from Vriesland. The other twelve elders, including Jannes Vande Luyster, a leading person in the village of Zeeland, were once delegates to classis or were considered elders from prior service in their churches in the Netherlands.

The first question addressed in this document was: "What confession and form of government is held by the churches emigrating from the Netherlands, and settling in Michigan, and what is the state of their development?" The answer, in brief, was a traditional historical and confessional answer coming out of the history and theology of the old Gereformeerde Kerk of the Netherlands, which were cherished by the 1834 Seceders.

The second question was: "Do these churches desire to unite themselves with the Dutch Reformed Churches in the United States of North America?" The first paragraph of the answer is as follows:

> We have a deep sense of our need of the communion of saints. We abominate sectarianism. In harmony with God's Word, and from thorough convictions, we say Amen to the inspired utterance that the eye cannot say to the hand, nor the head to the foot: I have no need of thee; and we consider it an abomination to say: I am holier than thou. We therefore seek the highest possible union with God's Church, wherever upon earth she manifests herself, if so be, that she professes and knows the way of salvation. Yet, so much the more do we feel ourselves to be one with those churches which have the same formulas of faith, the same liturgy and form of government, and which advocate the truth of God against all error. *We have never considered ourselves to be other than a part of the*

28 Van Eyck, *Union of 1850*, 70-74.
29 One elder was misclassified as a deacon at the April classis minutes.

Dutch Reformed Church, and desire on this account to live in communion with those churches and to send our delegates to their ecclesiastical assemblies.[30]

The third question was: "Are those churches in want?" You bet they were, the document asserted. Hear the actual words of the document again:

We will not conceal our manifest wants; on the contrary, it surprises and grieves us that the tender interests of those churches of God which, by reason of multifarious distresses and restraints have fled from the Fatherland and sought a refuge in the wilds of the West, have, for a period of already more than two years, escaped the attention of those Dutch Churches of Christ Jesus, albeit their members landed upon your shores, passed through your cities, and were known as followers of the same standards of faith.

Nevertheless, with heartfelt gratitude, a gratitude which impels tears to our eyes, and which moves us to kiss the Provident Hand of God, we acknowledge and will ever acknowledge, the kind hand of fraternal fellowship extended to us, by some of God's children in particular, in the painful condition of our alienage, who, as we sat at your docks, intermingled with thousands of immigrants, were not ashamed of us, but afforded refreshment and relief to our souls. Never shall we forget, [and] ever will we, and our children coming after us, remember them and their reward shall be of that God, who preserveth the stranger, and of that Saviour Who with an eternal recompense will remember the smallest favor shown to the least of His brethren.

The report goes on to say:

The experience we have here gathered convinces us that the churches in the East, enjoying peace and plenty, have a tremendous and weighty responsibility imposed upon them, to support the weaker members of the Body of Christ, who, in the providence of God, are scattered as a salt among the immigrants, so that they may not sink away beneath a too heavy burden, and lose the precious ordinances of the church of God.[31]

---

[30] Italics added. Van Eyck, *Union of 1850*, 73.
[31] Ibid.

John Garretson

A reading of this very crucial document shows that rather than thinking that the union was forced upon the churches of the Classis of Holland, the case is that the colony's churches felt that they were *neglected* by the RCA and that it had not done enough for the poor fellow believers in the wilds of Michigan.

In response to the pleas of this document, the RCA sprang into action. Rev. John Garretson, secretary of the Board of Domestic Mission, wrote on 10 August 1849 that the RCA was sending $250 to the classis for disbursement as the classis deemed fit.[32] Van Raalte wrote the board on 11 September thanking it for the support it had sent.[33] Funds and goods began to flow to the colony churches from New York and New Jersey churches

32 Adrian Van Koevering, *Legends of the Dutch, The Story of a Mass Movement of Nineteenth Century Pilgrims* (Zeeland, Mich.: Zeeland Record Co., 1960), 513.
33 A letter of Albertus C. Van Raalte to the Board of Domestic Missions of the RCA, box 9, folder "Annual Board Reports," Board of Domestic Missions Correspondence, Archives of the RCA, New Brunswick, N.J.

from then on. In time, the First Reformed Church of Holland received a considerable amount from the east to fund the building of its structure.[34]

On 1 May 1850 Van Raalte was in Schenectady, New York, as a representative of the Classis of Holland to attend the meeting of the Particular Synod of Albany with the request to unite with it. Interestingly enough, the synod called into question the legality of the Classis of Holland because it had not been authorized to organize by a denomination but had organized itself. However, the particular synod commended the classis to the General Synod for admission and immediately began to offer the classis help in every way possible.

At the June meeting of the General Synod held in Poughkeepsie, New York, the special committee of the General Synod, under the chairmanship of Dr. John Knox, recommended the admission into the RCA of the Classis of Holland with its nine congregations, six ministers, and over nine hundred communicant members.[35] When the first statistics of the Holland Classis were published in the 1852 General Synod minutes, there were twelve churches, six ministers, 563 families, and a total membership of men, women, and children in the amount of 2,854 souls.[36]

Knox, in his report to the General Synod, spoke highly of the colonists:

> By their orderly and industrious habits, and especially by their consistent and exemplary Christian demeanor, they have already in their new home, won for themselves high commendation and given earnest of taking rank with the soundest and best portions of the community. Descended from the same time-honored [Netherlands Reformed] Church through which, in her palmier days, the Reformed Dutch Church of North America derived her cherished religious institutions and privileges, it was to be expected that we should naturally care for these exiles from the fatherland.[37]

Thus, the synod voted in the affirmative and the Classis of Holland was admitted into the Reformed Church in America.

---

34 *The Leader*, 31 August 1910.
35 *The Acts and Proceedings of the General Synod of the Reformed Protestant Dutch Church in North America,...1850*, 68-69.
36 *Acts and Proceedings of the General Synod of the Reformed Protestant Dutch Church in North America,...1852*, 201.
37 *Acts and Proceedings of the General Synod,...1850*, 69.

Questions Raised by the Union.

Why did the churches of the Holland Classis join the RCA, and in such a short time after arrival in America? Some claimed that Van Raalte, who clearly spearheaded the movement for union, and the members of the classis simply did not know enough about the RCA to unite with it so quickly. However, Van Raalte was a reader of the *Christian Intelligencer*. He was too bright not to have informed himself well about the RCA before the Union of 1850. Van Raalte had contact with ministers of the RCA who lived in Michigan. The Michigan Classis of the RCA, which was composed of six churches, had been organized during the 1840s. Rev. Andrew Taylor, who became a good friend of the colonists, was serving the First Reformed Church of Grand Rapids, which had been organized in 1840.[38]

Van Raalte also read a copy of the "Digest of the Printed Minutes of the General Synod of the Reformed Protestant Dutch Church from the years 1794 to 1848."[39] Since Thomas De Witt was chair of the committee which produced the document in 1848, he would have made sure that Van Raalte obtained a copy. The digest, sixty-seven pages long and published in small print (pp. 339-406) detailed the essence and substance of the RCA. We know that Van Raalte had his own copy because his son Dirk showed the dog-eared copy to William O. Van Eyck.[40] Thus, in the years from late 1846 to June 1850, Van Raalte learned a great deal about the RCA. He clearly did not go into the union blindly, nor did the members of the classis. One can always, of course, raise the question how long the courtship should have been between the Classis of Holland and the RCA, just as we who are parents wonder how long our children should be in a courtship before they marry.

Why the RCA Courted the Classis of Holland and Wanted Union

It is possible that the RCA invited the colonists to unite with it because the RCA had very hard going in western church planting. James Romeyn, in his report of 1847, said it was difficult to conquer the West for the Reformed

---

38 Van Eyck, *Union of 1850*, 23.
39 *Acts and Proceedings of the General Synod of the Reformed Protestant Dutch Church in North America,…1848*, Appendix, 339-406.
40 Van Eyck, *Union of 1850*, 22.

Church but it was imperative to form a plan of action. Indeed,[41] nearly all of the forty plus churches founded by the RCA in the Middle West for American non-Dutch people during the middle of the nineteenth century failed and are no longer in existence. Only four exist to this day.

Adding Holland Classis to the rolls of the General Synod gave the RCA a great growth spurt. In a short time, the classis included all the Dutch immigrant congregations in the Middle West including Wisconsin, Iowa, and Illinois. By 1900, the number of RCA churches in the Middle West, both Dutch immigrant congregations and the American Reformed churches in the Michigan and Illinois classes, numbered 179 in eight classes. Moreover, even though RCA congregations in New York and New Jersey had Van Raalte knocking at their doors very soon after the union asking for funds for the Holland Academy, then Hope College, then for theological education which evolved into the institution of Western Seminary, the Reformed Church in time gained four of its five existing institutions through the Union of 1850: Hope College and Western Theological Seminary, Holland, Michigan; Central College, Pella, Iowa; and Northwestern College, Orange City, Iowa.

However, the most far-reaching effect of the Union of 1850 may be that the RCA continues to exist. The RCA attempted a merger with the German Reformed Church in the 1890s, only to have that attempt aborted by the Dutch immigrant congregations in the Middle West. Every merger attempted with the Presbyterians through the years was prevented by Dutch immigrant congregations of Afscheiding lineage in the Middle West. The descendants of the Afscheiding who voted to merge with the RCA in 1850 have vetoed every merger or union attempt since then. We will leave history to judge whether that is good or not.

A different kind of result of the Union of 1850 is that after the Christian Reformed Church became a viable denomination, almost all of its new congregations developed in communities where Dutch RCA congregations were already located: Holland and Grand Rapids, Michigan; South Holland, Roseland, and Chicago, Illinois; and Pella, Iowa, among others. The CRC did not start its congregations *de novo*, so to speak, but often developed out of established Reformed Church communities, where it offered an alternative to the RCA way of church life.

41 *Acts and Proceedings of the General Synod of the Reformed Protestant Dutch Church in North America,...1847*, 190-196.

The RCA has always considered that the union of the Classis of Holland with the Reformed Church in America in 1850 was a good move on the part of the Classis of Holland: it brought many benefits to the Holland colony, and the Holland Classis churches brought much to the RCA. Soon, however, voices were raised in opposition of this union, and, in a few years, the Secession of 1857 took place in protest of the union.[42]

---

[42] Van Raalte never veered from the position he took in 1850 about the union with the Reformed Dutch Church. When he and his wife made a return trip to the Netherlands in 1866 to visit family members and friends, he attended the synod of the Christelijke Afgescheidene Gereformeerde Kerk, where he was questioned about that union. Van Raalte was reported in the minutes to have said that the Reformed Dutch Church "is, with the exception of certain practices that spring from the character of the country, like the Gereformeerde Kerk in the Netherlands before 1816 in doctrine, discipline and worship. It recognizes the confessions of our Church as the expression of its faith and governs itself according to the church order of Dordt."

The minutes further summarize Van Raalte as saying that "that Church maintains no fellowship with Churches of whose orthodoxy they were not convinced".... As a result, the Congregation that emigrated from here to America felt themselves constrained to join that Church. As for the ecclesiastical secession, that developed because of the various elements that emigrated to North America and was the result not of unorthodoxy but of special causes."

Handelingen van de Synode der Christelijk Afgescheidene Gereformeerde Kerk in Nederland, 1866 (Kampen: S. van Velzen, Jr., 1866), 955-957. Translation by Dr. Henry ten Hoor.

III
1857
Secession Again:
Origins of the
Christian Reformed Church

The Secession of 1857 is loaded with emotional freight. William Van Eyck in his book *Landmarks of the Reformed Fathers* declared that the Seceders "were completely in error"; they had no "right under Reformed doctrine and practice" to call the Reformed Church in America a "corrupt and false church" and to name their rival body the True Dutch Reformed Church.[1] Henry Beets, a leading cleric in the Christian Reformed Church in the early twentieth century and its first historian, answered Van Eyck. The Secession of 1857 was merely a "return" to the standpoint of 1849, that is, the true church of 1834, said Beets.[2]

1   William O. Van Eyck, *Landmarks of the Reformed Fathers: Or What Dr. Van Raalte's People Believed* (Grand Rapids: Reformed Press, 1922), 24-25.
2   Henry Beets, *The Christian Reformed Church: Its Roots, History, Schools and Mission Work, A.D. 1857 to 1946* (Grand Rapids: Baker Book House, 1946), 59-60, 68-70. This book is an abridged English version of his earlier *De Chr. Geref. Kerk in N.A.: Zestig Jaren van Strijd en Zegen* (Grand Rapids: Grand Rapids Printing Co., 1918). A complete English translation, "Christian Reformed Church in N.A.," in 3 volumes, is available in the Calvin College Archives, Grand Rapids, Mich.

Calvin College Archives

Henry Beets

Both apologists resorted to polemics. Of course, the RCA was not as un-Reformed as the seceders of 1857 proclaimed, nor was the fledgling CRC as completely in error as its RCA critics charged. Theologian John Kromminga declared in a lecture at Pillar Christian Reformed Church twenty-five years ago, to a gathering of delegates representing both RCA and CRC churches, that 1834 was "much more defensible" than 1857.[3] But this point of view reflects our times and not those of 1834-1857.

The purpose of this chapter is to describe the 1857 schism and founding of the CRC from a historical rather than a theological perspective. The theological questions posed in chapter 2 (i.e., "What constitutes the true church?" and "What is the difference between the true and an apostate church?") are not amenable to direct answers. Historical questions are more easily answered. Instead of debating *whether* the RCA was apostate in 1850, we ask *why* some Dutch immigrants in Michigan believed that it was so and acted on that belief.

The central issue the Dutch immigrants faced was that of Americanization. Would they remain faithful disciples of the 1834 Secession leaders, de Cock,

[3] John H. Kromminga, "What Happened in 1857?" *Reformed Review* 27 (winter 1974): 112-118.

van Velzen, and Brummelkamp, in a strange land and keep their ties to the Seceder Church, or would they cut themselves loose and quickly integrate into American Reformed Christianity? Van Raalte pushed them in the direction of assimilation and a minority refused to go along. It is useful to know *who* made up that minority and *what* their complaints were. That may tell us something about why they seceded.

Cultural historians have arrived at the insightful conclusion that controversies over fine points of religious doctrine and practice in Protestant immigrant communities, such as the subject of this chapter, were a form of infighting that was incomprehensible to outsiders. The conflicts were very useful to immigrants, however, for the debates enabled them to build walls and define boundaries against the outside world. The Dutch Reformed squabbles in the Holland colony set the cultural boundaries of the community.[4] Religious scholars have also discovered recently that secessions, however problematic they might be, increase rather than decrease total church membership.[5] One can also argue that immigrants are better served by having a choice between a slower or a faster track to Americanization.

The schism of 1857 had a distinct 1834 flavor because the issues were brought over in the baggage of the immigrants themselves. Historical events always have antecedents. The Secession of 1834, which is described in chapter 1, brought to the fore issues and personalities that directly affected the 1857 schism. Many of the same players were involved. But 1857 was not an exact parallel of 1834 because the people in the Holland colony were living in a foreign land.

Precursors of Secession—Union of 1850

The Dutch immigrants from the outset were of two minds, one separatist and oriented to the Christian Seceded Church in the homeland, and the

4 Rob Kroes, *The Persistence of Ethnicity: Dutch Calvinist Pioneers in Amsterdam, Montana* (Urbana: University of Illinois Press, 1992), 100-103; Lawrence J. Taylor, *Dutchmen on the Bat: The Ethnohistory of a Contractual Community* (Philadelphia: University of Pennsylvania Press, 1983), 24-27; Hans Krabbendam, "Serving the Dutch Community: A Comparison of the Patterns of Americanization in the Lives of Two Immigrant Pastors [Bernardus de Bey and Roelof T. Kuiper]" (M.A. thesis, Kent State University, 1989), 136-137.
5 "Study Finds Churches that Split Survive," *Grand Rapids Press*, 8 March 1997; Roger Finke and Rodney Stark, *The Churching of America, 1776-1990: Winners and Losers in our Religious Economy* (New Brunswick, N.J.: Rutgers University Press, 1992).

other ecumenical and desirous of reaching out to fellow Reformed believers in the new homeland. Initially in 1848, the Dutch Seceder congregations in western Michigan, led by Rev. Albertus Van Raalte, created an independent church organization, Holland Classis, which the leaders considered to be an extension of the Seceded church in the Netherlands.[6] Within two years, however, the classis agreed to merge its one thousand members with the RCA, centered in New York and New Jersey.

The initiative clearly came from the RCA, which was heavily committed to expanding into the Midwest but was finding the task extremely difficult. The Dutch immigrants, who would soon number in the tens of thousands, could be the nucleus for that church planting work. As mentioned in the previous chapter, Rev. Isaac N. Wyckoff of Albany, New York, came to Holland in June 1849 as a representative of the RCA Board of Domestic Missions to encourage a merger.[7]

Wyckoff intended to meet only with the ministers on Saturday, present the board's proposal for merger, and then leave on Monday. But Van Raalte could not assemble the men on such short notice and persuaded Wyckoff to remain for a hastily convened classical meeting on Monday, May 4. On that occasion, "a great crowd" assembled, probably under the trees between Holland and Zeeland near Elder Broek's house. This was a central point in the settlement and the usual meeting place of the classis in those days. Here

---

6 I relied heavily in this section on John Kromminga, *The Christian Reformed Church: A Study in Orthodoxy* (Grand Rapids: Baker Book House, 1949), 23-39; D.H. Kromminga, *The Christian Reformed Tradition* (Grand Rapids: Wm. B. Eerdmans, 1943), 98-116; Albert Hyma, *Albertus C. Van Raalte and his Dutch Settlements in the United States* (Grand Rapids: Wm. B. Eerdmans, 1947), 193-238, Henry S. Lucas, *Netherlanders in America: Dutch Immigration to the United States and Canada, 1789-1950* (Ann Arbor: University of Michigan Press, 1955; reprint, Grand Rapids: Wm. B. Eerdmans, 1989), 506-515; Adriaan Van Koevering, *Legends of the Dutch: The Story of a Mass Movement of Nineteenth Century Pilgrims* (Zeeland, Mich.: Zeeland *Record*, 1960), 487-598; *Classis Holland Minutes 1848-1858* (Grand Rapids: Wm. B. Eerdmans, 1950); "Minutes of the Highest Assembly of the Christian Reformed Church, 1857-1880"(English translation, Calvin College Archives—hereafter cited as "CRC Classis Minutes").

7 Wyckoff's report on his visit is in Henry S. Lucas, *Dutch Immigrant Memoirs and Related Writings*, 2 vols. (Assen, the Netherlands: Van Gorcum, 1955; reprint, Grand Rapids: Wm. B. Eerdmans, 1997), 1:449-457. Wyckoff had already in September 1848 asked to attend a meeting of Holland Classis on behalf of the RCA, but the congregations were too preoccupied with survival to consider the invitation. *Classis Holland Minutes 1848-1858*, 26-27; Beets, "Christian Reformed Church in N.A.," 1:58-69, esp. 60.

all the ministers and many elders and interested members received Wyckoff "literally with a shout of joy," as he reported to RCA headquarters.[8]

Several weeks after Wyckoff's visit, and after discussions presumably had taken place in the congregations, Revs. Van Raalte, Cornelius Van der Meulen, Marten Ypma, and Seine Bolks, plus twenty elders, convened a second meeting at Van Raalte's home.[9] Here they signed a statement, dated 10 July 1849 and written by Van Raalte, that expressed the desire to "live in communion" with the RCA. This statement is the only poll on the question, and the signatories are worth considering. By congregation, thirteen of the twenty-four signatories were from Zeeland, seven represented Friesland, three were from Overisel, and one—Van Raalte himself—was from Holland. No church leader signed for the Graafschap, South Holland, Drenthe, and Grand Rapids congregations, including Rev. Hendrik G. Klijn of Graafschap and K.S. Vander Schuur (Ver Schuur) of South Holland. Nor did any elder from Van Raalte's congregation in Holland sign the statement, which is most surprising.[10] As it stands, this crucial document does not appear to speak for

8 No minutes of this unscheduled classis meeting exist, but Van Raalte kept notes and Wyckoff wrote a formal report, which was circulated nationally. See Beets, "Christian Reformed Church in N.A.," 1:61-62; William C. Van Eyck, *The Union of 1850* (Grand Rapids: Wm. B. Eerdmans, 1950), 70.

9 The question of whether Holland Classis convened only on 4 June 1849 with Wyckoff, or whether it met again later in June or even on 10 July in order to vote on the formal statement filed with the classis and dated 10 July 1849, is a very controversial one. Beets, "Christian Reformed Church in N.A.," 1:60-69, recognizes only one meeting and bases his view of the hasty and illegal nature of the proceedings on that fact. Van Eyck, *Union of 1850*, 32-33, 70-71, makes the more persuasive case for two meetings and for the deliberative nature of the process.

10 The document and list of signatories is in many publications, such as Van Eyck, *Union of 1850*, 74, which I compared with Holland Classis minutes. The three lay leaders—Johannes Kaboord, Jannis Vande Luyster, and Jan Steketee—of the Zeeland group migration of 1847 supported union, as did elders Jan Boes, Albert Borgers, Adriaan Glerum, Johannes Hoogesteger, Jan Kruit, Jan Van Bree, Jan Vander Werp, Johannes G. Van Hees, and Marinus Westrate. The Vriesland signers were Hendrik W. Dam, Klaas J. De Vree, E. Zylstra, G. De Groot, S. Kaslander, and Hessel O. Yntema. Overisel signers were elders Jan Lankheet and Gerrit J. Wolterink. Why Zeelanders and Frisians led the drive to union merits study. A biography of Ypma is Jelle Ypma, *Ds. Marten Annes Ypma, 1810-1863: Van Minnertsga (Friesland) naar Vriesland (Michigan)* (Leeuwarden: Gereformeerde Kerk, Hallum, and *Friesch Dagblad*, 1986). Although trained in the northern party, Ypma in Michigan identified with Van Raalte's southern party.

the colony as a whole.[11]

This fact concerned Van Raalte greatly, according to an eyewitness. "Brethren, this is wrong. I warn you. If it later proves to be a mistake, then it is our fault. If we refer this to the congregations, and it is a mistake, then it is also the fault of the congregations." It appears that the classis heeded this warning and did consult with the individual consistories. On 30 July 1849 the Vriesland consistory met and approved the 10 July union statement. No minutes survive of such a meeting in any of the other churches of the classis, but it is likely that they were likewise consulted on this critical issue. A later report, for example, stated that a majority of the Graafschap consistory opposed the union.[12]

Nine months later, in April 1850, the classis commissioned Van Raalte to attend the Particular Synod at Albany with instructions "to give and to ask for all necessary information which may facilitate the desired union."[13] This somewhat ambiguous statement about a "desired union" is as close to a formal decision as the classis ever took on the merger. After Van Raalte's most cordial welcome at the May synodical meeting, that body and subsequently the General Synod agreed "that the Classis of Holland be received under the care of General Synod." This consummated the union, without further debate or action by the churches of Holland Classis. The classis never voted on a specific motion to join the RCA, either before or after the synodical meetings, but it did state officially in April 1851, that the union was "a source of joy and gratitude."[14]

---

[11] In *Union of 1850*, Van Eyck, an apologist for the RCA, tries to explain the dearth of signatures on the so-called "Report of the Twenty-four" by suggesting that the twenty-four were "a sort of committee" acting for the larger conference of 4 June or as the Classis of Holland again in session (71).

[12] The Van Raalte quote is reported by Tede Ulberg in "Notes on the First Settlers in the Dutch Kolonie in Michigan," Lucas, *Dutch Immigrant Memoirs and Related Writings*, 1:287; Van Eyck, *Union of 1850*, 32-33. Says Van Eyck, "Vriesland's case, again, is in harmony with the spirit of 1849, and it requires contemporaneous record evidence of the strongest kind to break the presumption that the Vriesland rule was followed in the other colonial churches." Unfortunately, the minutes of Holland, Zeeland, Graafschap, and Overisel of these days are lost. The Graafschap church stance is noted in Beets, "Christian Reformed Church in N.A.," 1:70.

[13] *Classis Holland Minutes*, 36-37.

[14] Hyma, *Van Raalte*, 202-205; *The Acts and Proceedings of the General Synod of the Reformed Protestant Dutch Church in North America,...1850*, 69; *Classis Holland Minutes*, 52.

"So the union was an accomplished fact," said Henry Beets. "The bond of ecclesiastical marriage was consummated between two parties who had known one another for only a short time, who did not understand one another's language, who had not had sufficient time to nourish mutual appreciation—that indispensable foundation for a permanent loving marriage." The whole process ran counter to Reformed church polity and was "illegal."[15]

Viewed pragmatically, the decision was a natural outgrowth of strengthening ties that had developed even prior to emigration between the Seceder leaders and the American church.[16] The old Dutch Reformed met the young Dutch Reformed at customs; provided temporary lodging; gave food, clothing, and money to the destitute; and loaned several thousand dollars to purchase land. Monies and goods continued to flow to the colony and helped it survive the difficult first years. Needless to say, these acts of kindness engendered much goodwill among the first contingents of Dutch dissenters during their "time of troubles."

While the aid from the East was much appreciated, many in the colony were very uneasy concerning union with that Americanized denomination, of which they knew so little. A merger would also distance them over time from their roots in the 1834 Secession movement, with its mentality of separatism and suspicion of autocratic synods. That the colonial leaders shared these concerns is acknowledged in Wyckoff's report to his synod (see chapter 2), and it can also be inferred from the fact that the nine churches comprising Holland Classis insisted on joining the RCA as a unit, rather than being fused with the eight congregations in the American-speaking Classis of Michigan that had been organized in 1847. Keeping the Dutch way was important.

Graafschap and South Holland—Revs. K. S. Vander Schuur and Jacob R. Schepers

Even before the Union of 1850, secession movements within Holland Classis had begun in two of the seven congregations, Graafschap and

---

15 Beets, "Christian Reformed Church in N.A.," 1:65-69 (quote 65). As explained earlier, Beets based his conclusion on the one meeting assumption.
16 Van Eyck, *Landmarks*, chap. 25.

Drenthe, which provided a kind of dress rehearsal for 1857.[17] In the Graafschap church was a faction from the provinces of Drenthe and Overijssel living in the hamlet of South Holland, led by wealthy landowner and elder Harm Jan Smit of Hoogeveen, Drenthe. In 1848, the faction called as its pastor Rev. K.S. Vander Schuur, a student of de Cock who pastored the Hoogeveen Seceder church for five years until being placed under censure in 1845. Smit was a champion of Vander Schuur. Even though the South Holland call was totally irregular, because the group acted on its own without obtaining the permission of the classis, yet the classis acquiesced. The colony needed preachers desperately, and Vander Schuur came with proper credentials, having made his peace with the Seceder denomination (who likely saw his call to America as a satisfactory resolution).[18]

When Rev. Klijn, a student of Scholte, arrived from the Netherlands in 1849 in answer the Graafschap church's call to be its first pastor, he was surprised to find Vander Schuur already serving the congregation's South Holland band. To head off conflict, the classis induced Vander Schuur to leave for the Grand Haven church and then for Sheboygan. This frustrated the South Holland group, who made life miserable for Klijn, and he left for the Milwaukee church. The Utrecht-born Klijn also could not adapt to the hardships of pioneer living, and his centrist theological orientation did not fit well in the Cocksian stronghold of Graafschap.[19]

17 Smit affiliated his congregation with the Associate Reformed denomination: Hendrik J. Prakke, *Drenthe in Michigan* (Assen: Van Gorcum, 1948); Roelof Diephuis, "Reminder of Rev. Roelof Smit and His Life" (in Dutch), *Missionary Monthly* 13 (March 1941), translation by Peter H. Bouma in Herrick Library, Holland, Mich.; and four articles in Lucas, *Dutch Immigrant Memoirs and Related Writings*, 1:253-71; *Seventy-fifth Anniversary of the Drenthe Christian Reformed Church, 1882-1957* (Drenthe, Mich.,1957), 7-9, in Calvin College Archives.

18. The South Holland Reformed (later Scottish Presbyterian) Church stood at the corner of present day Michigan Avenue and 32nd Street in Holland (two miles east and one mile north of the Graafschaap church). The congregation was composed of the families Beekman (Beckman), Harm Bremer, P.A. Kleis, Hendrik Manting, Plasman, Harm Jans Smit, and Derk Zaalmink. Manting, Smit, and Zaalmink served as elders. *Classis Holland Minutes*, 92; "A Church That Few if Any Here Knew About," undated clipping in *Holland City News* in author's possession. Harm Jans Smit patented five tracts, totaling 737 acres, at the Ionia Public Land Office in 1848 and 1849, situated south of the village of Holland (Book of Original Entries, Government Land Office, Ionia, Michigan, in Federal Bureau of Land Management, Washington). I am indebted to Richard Harms for this information.

19 *Honderd Veertig Jaar Gemeenten en Predikanten van de Gereformeerde Kerken in Nederland* (n.p.: Algemeen Bureau van de Gereformeerde Kerken en

In 1851 Harm Smit and the South Holland church induced Jacob R. Schepers, an 1848 immigrant who was studying for the ministry under Rev. C. Vander Meulen at Zeeland and had been licensed to "exhort" by Holland Classis, to come as an unordained minister. Schepers, a native of Hijken (near Beilen) in the Province of Drenthe, had begun his ministerial apprenticeship in 1840 in the parsonage of de Cock's disciple, Walter Kok,

Nederland, 1974), 249, 227; Edward T. Corwin, *A Manual of the Reformed Church in America, 1628-1902,* 4th ed. (New York: Board of Publication of the Reformed Church in America, 1902), 814, 554. Klijn, born in Utrecht and a follower of J.H.F. Kohlbrugge and student of Scholte, was a leader who served Seceder churches throughout the province of Utrecht based at Kockengen (1839-1845) and throughout the province of Zeeland based at Middelburg (1845-1849). See A. Graafhuis, "De Afscheiding in de Stad Utrecht," in *Aspecten van de Afscheiding,* ed. A. de Groot and P.L. Schram (Franeker, the Netherlands: Wever, 1984), 45-52.

Rev. David McNeish, pastor of the Constantine, Michigan, Reformed Church, visited the Holland colony and learned from Van Raalte about the events at South Holland and Drenthe, which he reported by letter to John Garretson, director of RCA Domestic Missions. This important letter deserves to be quoted at length. McNeish reported that a "man of some property," an elder in the Graafschap church living in South Holland who was a friend of Vander Schuur

> wrote a [letter of] call, as if emanating from the church, signed it himself & induced one other man, also a member of the Consistory, to sign it & discretely transmitted this to Holland. The Classis in Holland [The Netherlands] were surprised to receive a call for such a man [since they had previously censured him]. But after deliberating on the subject & especially after receiving the humble acknowledgements of Van Scheur & his promises of future good behavior, they consented to restore him & send him here with clean papers. The Church here [at Graafschap], as I have said, had been kept in ignorance of this movement. But being anxious to procure the services of a minister of the gospel, they made out a call in constitutional form on Dominie Kline. This also was transmitted to Holland. He accepted the same & arrived here. But what was his surprise to find that Van Scheur had preceded him to the same church. This, of course, produced trouble. The Classis here did all that was in their power to compose the trouble. Van Scheur was induced to accept a call made to him by a church across the Lake in Sheboygan, I think, but after he left, the few who had been the means of his coming here, were not satisfied to remain in quietness. This made it uncomfortable for Dom. Kline & he too left them, having accepted a call from our Holland Church in Milwaukee.

McNeish to Garretson, 11 December 1853, box 11, fldr. Nov.-Dec. 1853, Correspondence of the Board of Domestic Missions of the Reformed Church, Archives of the RCA, New Brunswick, N.J. I used a copy in the Joint Archives of Holland, Holland, Mich. See also *Classis Holland Minutes,* 34-35, 43-44, 64-65. The "man of some property" was clearly Harm Jans Smit of Hoogeveen.

Calvin College Archives

Walter A. Kok   *Jacob R. Schepers*

at Hoogeveen. Fellow students were Roelof Smit, Koene Vanden Bosch, and Willem H. Frieling. All four later became leaders in the Christian Reformed Church. Thus, Walter Kok is the spiritual father of the Christian Reformed Church even though he never emigrated.[20]

Neither Schepers nor the South Holland elders officially informed his pastor, Vander Meulen, or Holland Classis of this "call." Van Raalte attributed the oversight to Schepers's over-eagerness for a position. "Temptation overcame him." When the church asked the classis to install Schepers, it refused without first ordaining him, which regular church polity required.[21] Schepers harbored objections against the RCA and apparently

---

[20] Those from Drenthe were more southern minded, but Schepers was influenced more by the northern-minded way of thinking. Prakke, *Drenthe in Michigan*, 55-56; M. Bouwens, "Wijlen Ds. J. Schepers" (obituary), *Yearbook 1899 of the Christian Reformed Church*, 77-80 (translation, Calvin College Archives). For a "considerable time" in 1850 Schepers served as the preaching elder for a small group at Groningen, who were members of the Zeeland congregation but desirous of having their own church. Holland Classis would not allow the needless proliferation of small, weak congregations, and the group withered away. See Abraham Stegeman, "Historical Sketch of Groningen," in Lucas, *Dutch Immigrant Memoirs*, 1:164-66; *Classis Holland Minutes*, 48-51.

[21] Schepers's strident letter of 18 February 1852 to the classis and Van Raalte's biting reply of 20 February 1852 are in *Holland Classis Minutes*, 91-93.

did not want to face the classical candidacy exam. Having become a friend of the Associate Reformed Church pastor in Gun Plains, Michigan, which was a conservative, psalm-singing Scottish Calvinist body, Schepers in 1852 obtained ordination as an evangelist in that Presbytery, and the South Holland church seceded.[22]

---

22 Again, McNeish's letter is important. He says that Schepers "dreaded" the classical examination and

> took no notice of their answer further than to transmit an imperative demand for ordination. This, of course, could not be complied with. But this same Schepers, had a brother who had been working among the members of an Associate Reformed Church just a mile from where we stayed all night in Gun Plains, when on our way to Grand Rapids. These very excellent people had learned that the Hollanders like themselves sang only the Psalms. They had not neglected to enlarge on the great sin of our Churches in singing Hymns, the mere composition of sinful men. The young man returned to Graafschap full of this new discovery. The young man who sought ordination at the hands of the Classis & was refused unless he submitted to an examination, is next heard of knocking loudly at the doors of the Associate Presbytery for admission there, that he may be found in the bosom of a Pure Church, where only old John Rouse is the standard of sacred music. He tells them that he has learned with horor (sic) that the Churches in New York "sing human compositions" & that the Classis of Holland has joined such a sinful body, but that he can not consent to such union. He is therefore before them with his original license from Holland & also with a call from a church in Graafschap, that he craved admission to their pure body for his church & for himself admission & ordination. They looked at his License, which was no other than the aforesaid permission to exhort, but it was in the Holland language & of course was as intelligible as if it had been written in Choctow to these Schotsmen. But one thing they knew & that was that they were sound in Psalm singing, & according to their logic, must also be in Theology. So they admitted the Church & ordained this poor ignorant young man, their pastor. This then is the history of one of these *Presbyterian Holland Churches*.

McNeish to Garretson, 11 December 1853; *Classis Holland Minutes*, 28, 62, 79-82, 91-93, 99-100. The Associate Reformed Presbyterian Church examined Schepers at a classical assembly in Caledonia, Michigan (Bouwens, "Schepers," 77). This denomination, which merged into the United Presbyterian Church in 1858, maintained the ban on hymn singing for 142 years until 1946, when in a close vote the synod made it optional (*Missionary Monthly* 51 [Nov. 1946]: 332). In 1858 Harm Smit, the leader of the South Holland group, had a falling out with the Scottish church and was censured, according to Graafschap CRC elder Jacob de Frel. Smit, reportedly, then tried unsuccessfully to return to the Reformed Church. The Graafschap church convened a special consistory meeting on 23 July 1858 to deal with the matter (Graafschap CRC consistory minute book).

Western Seminary Collection,
Joint Archives of Holland

Roelof H. Smit

Drenthe and Rev. Roelof Smit

A second precursor of 1857 was the trial and deposition by Holland Classis in 1853 of Rev. Roelof Smit of Rouveen, Province of Overijssel, who emigrated in 1851 to pastor the Michigan congregation. This church had a history of factiousness and strife, which was caused by a spirit of clannishness already rife in the old country that pitted people from the western Staphorst region against those from the eastern area of Emmen and Sleen. Indeed, already in 1849 the classis had to deal with the Drenthe consistory's expulsion and later the excommunication of elder Jan Hulst of Staphorst.

Smit, who was trained in the de Cock northern party of the Seceders rather than with the southern party of Van Raalte, came into this troubled place and aligned himself with his compatriot Hulst and with the like-minded Schepers, whom he soon visited. Within two weeks of Smit's arrival in Michigan, he reportedly had "already slandered Van Raalte." He also absented himself from a regular classis meeting in April 1853 without giving notice. This meeting was mainly devoted to the controversial question of founding a separate Christian day school, the English Academy, for which

Drenthe Scottish Church

Van Raalte offered ten choice town lots in Holland and a New York RCA philanthropist granted $500 in seed money. Both gifts were contingent on the churches of the classis endorsing the school, which the body did unanimously. Smit, apparently, opposed a school that would put children on the fast track to Americanization, even if it was Christian.[23]

Smit and Hulst insisted on keeping the festival days—Christmas, Good Friday, Resurrection, and Pentecost—which was mandated by the Dort church order but which Holland Classis made optional on the flimsy grounds that it was impractical to force busy farmers to assemble for mid-week services. Smit even celebrated the Lord's Supper on such days, which did not sit well with the members who opposed special services and thus missed out on the sacrament.[24]

23 Prakke, *Drenthe in Michigan*, 55-58; *Classis Holland Minutes*, 112-113, 126, 128.
24 *Holland Classis Minutes*, 60, 118-119. McNeish also reported on Smit in his letter to Garretson.

He soon began to give them great trouble by insisting on the strict observance of certain feast or *Pussegete* days. The members of Consistory told him that they would not object to his having public worship on those days, but that they would not permit him to *compel* the attendance of the members of Church on such occasions. This however he demanded.

In 1853 five men from the Drenthe church complained to the classis that their pastor "promotes factions, acts arbitrarily, thrusts aside and oppresses the former leaders of the church, and promotes to office those who are ignorant." More seriously, they charged that Smit "tried to make the church secede," claiming that Holland Classis was "sold to the Old Dutch Church by Van Raalte for a good purse of money."[25]

Smit sought to defend himself before the classis by explaining that he had to act independently; otherwise his congregation would have said, "See, he is already swallowing another of Van Raalte's pills." Smit condemned the "popist lust for lordship" by the classis and refused to yield an inch. The body "rebuked him for his arbitrary and carnal conduct in oppressing the church" and urged both he and his critics to forgive and be reconciled. Within days

When they absented themselves he proceeded to the infliction of suspension & even excommunication for their neglect of the ordinances of grace. He took care always to celebrate the Com. of the Lord's Supper at such times. When he had carried matters thus far, the church appealed for redress to their Classis. The brethren, however, preferred (sic) to go & use their best offices for healing the troubles in an unofficial capacity. They supposed that they had succeeded, for he made proper apologies for his past conduct & promises of future amendment. The Brethren had no sooner left than he began to carry things with as high a hand as ever. He even went so far as to read the names of one of his Elders from the Pulpit one day, as an excommunicated person. The Consistory learned for the first time from the Pulpit that one of their number had suffered the highest penalty of the Church. Mr. Smith did it of his own mere motion. In the meantime the Classis had taken up the whole matter. They found, however, that he was a man whose *word* or *promise* could not be relied upon. Indeed they were compelled to proceed to his deposition from the ministry—'a long chain' of lying is one of the charges preferred & proved. But now his conscience became tender in relation to Psalm singing and he tells the Associate Presbytery that he claims admission among them on his papers from Holland. That they were not to inquire about his connection with the Classis here, that he had protested against all their acts in relation to himself, that they were in fact a body that was seeking his destruction by oppressive sentences, & above all that they had erred from the faith by joining a Church which *sang human* compositions, etc. Would you believe it? These men actually received him as if a minister in good & regular standing on his presentation of his papers he had brought with him from Holland. Why Classis had not retained them I do not know. They knew him to be lying under the excommunication of the Classis for crimes which had been proved against him. It makes me sick at heart to write this & I cannot make any comment.

[25] *Classis Holland Minutes*, 34, 42, 45-46, 116-139.

Original Drenthe Church

Smit advocated secession for his followers in a raucous public meeting attended by elders from every church in the classis. In May 1853 Smit and two-thirds of the Drenthe church seceded, and, like Schepers's South Holland congregation, they too joined the Associate Reformed Church, known popularly as the "Schotse Kerk."[26] Smit and Schepers together also organized a "Secession" congregation in Grand Haven in 1855. Kromminga called Smit "an impossibly arbitrary and self-centered character," to which Van Raalte would readily have concurred. Yet, Smit pastored a very faithful

---

[26] McNeish to Garretson, 11 December 1853; *Classis Holland Minutes*, 117-139 (quotes 128, 129); Prakke, *Drenthe in Michigan*, 55-56. Another Seceder pastor, A.C. Tris, who immigrated in 1851 to serve a small Seceder congregation in Albany, New York, likewise refused to join the RCA, despite his close personal friendship with Wyckoff, and instead affiliated with the Associate Reformed Church. Matters of conscience for Tris were the RCA permitting of freemasons and slave holders as members, the use of hymns, and the rotation system of elders and deacons, besides other unspecified "points of difference." Like Hendrik P. Scholte, Tris had suffered too much in the Netherlands at the hands of synods to submit again. See A.C. Tris, *Sixty Years' Reminiscences and Spiritual Experiences in Holland and in the United States of America* (Lebanon, Penn.: Report Publishing Co., 1908), 108-109; Van Eyck, *Secession of 1850*, 19-20.

congregation which joined the CRC on his recommendation after his death in 1886.[27]

Jacob Duim, Independent Preacher of North Holland

A third secession took place in North Holland in 1855, led by Jacob Duim of Noordeloos, province of Zuid-Holland, who had emigrated with his parents in 1847 to South Holland, Illinois.[28] Families from this locale founded the colonies of Noordeloos and North Holland, Michigan. The Duim family brought a tradition of conventicle worship and distrust of Reformed churches that was common among Seceders.

In 1855 Jacob Duim resettled in North Holland, Michigan, and, though lacking formal training, "claimed to be a minister or teacher and in sole possession of the truth." He formed a conventicle and began conducting worship services, which drew most of the members of the local congregation that Van Raalte had organized in 1851. Duim accused Van Raalte of preaching the false doctrines of Jacob Arminius and condemned him and the other ministers in the classis as "Baal-leaders and not leaders, but deceivers." The ministers believe that Christians have "accepted" Christ but not that they have "received" him. "The fault is with the learned, not with the unlearned," agreed his correspondent, Paulus Den Bleyker. Duim promised to continue the reform of the church begun in 1834. "I still see a beam of light in Switzerland," he claimed, in reference to the Swiss *Réveil* that had sparked the Afscheiding.[29]

---

27 Kromminga, "What Happened in 1857," 115; Adriaan Keizer, "Drenthe's History to the Present," in Lucas, *Dutch Immigrant Memoirs and Related Writings*, 1:263; Beets, "Christian Reformed Church in N.A.," 2:125.

28 The Duim family arrived at New York from Amsterdam on the *Mississippi of Demerara* on 18 December 1847. Robert P. Swierenga, comp., *Dutch Immigrants in U.S. Ship Passenger Lists: An Alphabetical Listing by Family Heads and Independent Persons*, 2 vols. (Wilmington, Del.: Scholarly Resources, 1987), 1:267-68.

29 Pieter G. Van Tongeren, "North Holland," in Lucas, *Dutch Immigrant Memoirs*, 2:467; quotes in Herbert J. Brinks, "Church History via Kalamazoo, 1850-1860," *Origins* 16, no. 1 (1998): 37. Brink's important article draws heavily on new material in the Den Bleyker Family Papers, Bentley Historical Library, Ann Arbor. Gordon J. Spykman, *Pioneer Preacher Albertus Christian Van Raalte: A Study of His Sermon Notes* (Grand Rapids: Calvin College and Seminary, 1976) characterized Van Raalte's preaching as Calvinist and Reformed but bifurcated, with a "heavily intellectual emphasis on doctrine" in the tradition of Protestant scholasticism on one hand, "counterbalanced by an equally heavy emphasis on pietism on the other hand." Van Raalte's sermons thus created a "polar tension" between doctrinal "expositions" and pious "applications" (68-69).

Local History Department,
Kalamazoo Public Library

Paulus Den Bleyker

Duim's church at North Holland flourished for a time. In 1857 he declared: "I now feel that I have special instructions from the Lord to lead and oversee this flock. Attendance on Sunday has been larger than ever and the spirit is good." Duim catechized the young people on Sunday and instructed the young men's society on Wednesday evenings. But in the spirit of Anabaptism, he refused to baptize the children, apparently believing the parents to be spiritually immature: "the people are in the wilderness," he declared. When RCA pastor Engelbert C. Oggel came to North Holland in 1866, he found seventy-five unbaptized children. Oggel rejuvenated the church and managed to win all but five or six families away from Duim. Only two families remained loyal to him at his death in 1879.[30]

Gysbert Haan, Father of the 1857 Secession

Gysbert Haan, elder in the Vriesland church in 1849 and after 1853 elder in Grand Rapids, was another leader with strong opinions. He was a follower of Simon van Velzen and stood in the de Cock tradition. After worshiping for a time in the RCA churches of Albany and Rochester, Haan had in 1850 settled in western Michigan, where he brought reports of purported "irregularities" in the RCA. Haan charged that many ministers and elders

---

30 Van Tongeren, "North Holland," in Lucas, *Dutch Immigrant Memoirs*, 2:467; Brinks, "Church History via Kalamazoo," 38.

Gysbert Haan

held membership in "secret societies" (masonic lodges), churches practiced "open" (e.g. unregulated) Communion, used choirs in worship services to the detriment of congregational singing, sang "man-made" hymns rather than the Davidic psalms, and neglected catechetical preaching. At least one elder in Paterson did not present a single one of his children for baptism, Haan reported, in the belief that they should be free to choose for themselves as adults. Another elder rejected the doctrine of election, and a minister confessed to never having preached it, and so forth. More than any other individual, Haan's polemics, in the words of John Kromminga, "fed the fires of discontent."[31]

Haan and his fellow dissenters in west Michigan, Vanden Bosch, Duim, Schepers, and Smit, had another source of information about the perceived

31 John Kromminga, *Christian Reformed Church*, 32; D.H. Kromminga, *Christian Reformed Tradition*, 107-111; Fred E. Velders, "The Reformed Heritage and Historical Background Leading to the Founding of the Christian Reformed Church" (B.D. thesis, California Baptist Theological Seminary, 1953), 64-77. Gysbert Haan's account is his *Voice of One Slandered* (Grand Rapids: C. Nienhardt, 1871), translation by William K. Reinsma available in Calvin College Archives. See also R. John Hager, "Gysbert Haan, A Study in Alienation," *Reformed Journal* 13 (Nov. 1963): 7-10, 13 (Dec. 1963): 12-15, 14 (Jan. 1964): 15-18; and Peter Plug, "Gysbert Haan and the Secession of 1857," unpublished manuscript, Calvin College Archives. Forceful apologists for the Reformed Church in America of the events of 1850 and 1857 are Van Eyck, *Landmarks of the Reformed Fathers*; Nicholas H. Dosker, *De Hollandsche Gereformeerde Kerk in Amerika* (Nijmegen:P.J. Milborn, 1888), and Henry E. Dosker, *Levensschets van Rev. A.C. van Raalte, D.D.* (Nijkerk: C. C. Callenbach, 1893), 240-276.

apostasy in the RCA in the East. That was Rev. Jan Berdan, a pastor in the True Reformed Protestant Church that had seceded from the RCA in 1822. Berdan, in a lengthy letter to Den Bleyker, charged the RCA with "preaching universal atonement, man's natural ability to do good works, and with the practice of open communion tables." This letter circulated widely in west Michigan. Schepers read a Dutch translation to his Presbyterian congregation in South Holland, so none would doubt the reasons for his own actions.[32]

Haan's name appears regularly in the minutes of Holland Classis. In 1853 elder [William] Vande Luyster of Holland brought a letter from Milwaukee to the classis asking "whether it was lawful for a member of the church to be a Freemason." According to Haan, who was present, the dialogue went like this: Vande Luyster was asked, "'What is your purpose in bringing this matter to Classis?' 'None other,' he replied, 'than to hear the opinion of the brethren....' 'No,' was the response, 'you want to throw a bomb into the Dutch Reformed Church.'" At this Haan took the floor and said: "'Brethren, this evil, Freemasonry, is so prevalent in America that even many ministers are members of this order, and this, together with all the other un-Reformed matters that are present, makes it desirable, in my opinion, to exist here as a separate body, but connected with the Seceder church in the Netherlands, and to abandon the tie with the Dutch Reformed Church; what need do we have of it.'" Classis minutes show that the body took no official action about freemasonry, but they do report that "all look upon it as works of darkness, and thus unlawful for a (church) member." So the classis expressed its collective opinion in a "sense of the house" motion, and presumably consistories acted accordingly in counseling and disciplining members.[33]

In 1855 Haan protested to the classis that Van Raalte and Vander Meulen had recommended to their colleagues the popular tract of Rev. Richard Baxter, *Call to the Unconverted*, which contained Arminian sentiments of universal grace. That same year one of Van Raalte's own elders, charter member Abraham Krabshuis, had publicly accused Van Raalte and Bolks in the city newspaper of not preaching the catechism. The next year Haan

32 Brinks, "Church History via Kalamazoo," 37-38.
33 Consistory Minutes, February 1857, Graafschap Christian Reformed Church; *Classis Holland Minutes*, 144, 180, 182, 187-197, and passim; for the Holland Classis dialogue, see Roelof T. Kuiper, *A Voice from America about America* (1881), trans. E. R. Post (Grand Rapids: Wm. B. Eerdmans, 1970), 85.

brought another protest before the classis regarding alleged irregularities in an election of elders and deacons in the Spring Street congregation of Grand Rapids. He had earlier charged that the classis disobeyed the Dort church order by allowing inactive elders to hold office for life and by not requiring the observance of festival days.[34]

Underlying all of Haan's grievances was the suspicion that the RCA was tainted with heterodoxy, which charge the classis judged to be groundless. Both Vander Meulen and Van Raalte tried to dissuade him but failed. He was a troublemaker, they concluded, who manifested a "wrongness in his attitude of heart." In 1856 Haan withdrew from the RCA before the classis could discipline him. Other lay leaders left with him from the Grand Rapids, Holland, and Vriesland congregations[35]. Haan had posed the critical question: Why not abandon the tie to the RCA and remain linked to the Seceded Church in the Netherlands? Why not remain true to the Seceder principles?

Noordeloos and Rev. Koene Vanden Bosch

The subsequent arrival of new colonists fresh from the Netherlands brought reinforcements for Haan and the elders' position. Many, such as the Noordeloos congregation of Dominie Koene Vanden Bosch (1818-1897), could not appreciate the crucial help from the East in the early days. Vanden Bosch, a classmate of Schepers and Smit in Kok's parsonage in Hoogeveen, decried the Union of 1850 from the moment of his arrival in 1856. He had heard from dissatisfied brothers in Graafschap and Holland even before leaving the Netherlands and was particularly taken with Haan's complaints against the RCA. When Vanden Bosch voiced his concerns to the classis,

34 *Classis Holland Minutes,* 58-59, 61, 173, 182, 187-197. Haan's most important supporter in the Grand Rapids church was Jan Gelok, a follower of Rev. Ledeboer in the Reformed Churches under the Cross. Beets, "Christian Reformed Church in N.A.," 1:76. Krabshuis resigned as elder and withdrew from the Holland church 14 January 1856, joining the Graafschap congregation. He was the only leader among the house church advocates who joined the CRC. But after five years he concluded that Graafschap was not a true church and withdrew into religious isolation (Brinks, "Church History via Kalamazoo," 39, 40).
35 *Classis Holland Minutes,* 203-207, 225-226; Kromminga, *Christian Reformed Church,* 33, 37. Haan submitted his letter of resignation to the consistory meeting of Second Reformed Church 14 April 1856. Those joining Haan included Jan Gelok (Gelock), A. Van Hoven, P. Haan, G. Grootveld, and G.E.J. Ham. Elder H.W. Dam of the Vriesland church resigned 5 May 1856. Beets, "Christian Reformed Church in N.A.," 1:92.

Calvin College Archives

Koene Vanden Bosch

however, he was told, "We will not act on these matters, and in no way will you be able to get us to bring these matters to Synod."[36]

Interestingly, Vanden Bosch drew off some members of Jacob Duim's group in North Holland, which was just a few miles down the road. Vanden

36 Noordeloos Christian Reformed Church, *Centennial, 1857-1957*, 11, in Calvin College Archives. Vanden Bosch's parents and eight siblings emigrated in 1848 for religious freedom to Zeeland, but Vanden Bosch, the oldest, had remained behind because he was studying for the ministry under de Cock and then served a Seceder congregation in Noordeloos, Zuid Holland. In 1856 he emigrated with his family and twenty-nine members of his congregation to serve the Michigan congregation that Holland Classis had organized that year in anticipation of his coming. His father, Tamme, and other family members helped found the congregation. The quote about Holland Classis is in Henry Beets, "Ds. Koene Vanden Bosch, II, Life's History in America," *Gereformeerde Amerikaan*, April 1902, 183-192; a translation by Hero Bratt available at A. C. Van Raalte Institute, Holland, Mich. See memoir of his married sister, Grietje Boone, "Journey and Arrival of Tamme vanden Bosch," in Lucas, *Dutch Immigrant Memoirs and Related Writings*, 1:258-259; Lucas, *Netherlanders in America*, 148-149; *Classis Holland Minutes*, 198-199. For an excellent treatment of Vanden Bosch, see Herbert J. Brinks, "Religious Continuities in Europe and the New World," 209-223, in *The Dutch in America: Immigration, Settlement, and Cultural Change*, ed. Robert P. Swierenga (New Brunswick, N.J.: Rutgers University Press, 1985).

Bosch shared Duim's religious outlook but was trained and properly ordained by Holland Classis. Vanden Bosch, according to Duim, would have accepted a call from the Graafschap congregation in 1856, but it was conditional on him leading the church out of the denomination. "Bosch is still a friend of the *Keyzer*," Duim charged, referring to Van Raalte.[37] If true, the friendship was doomed.

Secession March-April 1857

The end result of the years of protests against the 1850 union decision was the creation of the True Dutch Reformed (later Christian Reformed) Church. In March and April 1857, two clerics—Vanden Bosch of Noordeloos and Klijn of Grand Rapids, together with members of four congregations— Noordeloos, Polkton, Grand Rapids, and Graafschap—decided by majority vote to withdraw from the Reformed Church in America and "return" to an independent status. A fifth church, Vriesland, joined them shortly. The use of the term "return" referred to a claim, based on a technicality, that the Union of 1850 was consummated illegally. The protesters sent their letters of secession to Holland Classis, which met in Zeeland 8 April 1857. This date is thus considered the birthday of the Christian Reformed Church. The withdrawal of the two clerics, it should be noted, followed by one year the departure of Haan and the other lay leaders in the spring of 1856. Just as in 1834, lay people sparked the secession movement of 1857.

Vanden Bosch's withdrawal letter to Holland Classis was biting, while Klijn's was irenic. Vanden Bosch declared that the RCA was not a "true church of Jesus Christ" because of the "abominable and church-destroying heresy and sins which are rampant" in it. To belong to a church infected with such "extreme wickedness" was unconscionable, Vanden Bosch declared, and "consequently, I renounce all fellowship with you and declare myself no longer to belong to you."[38]

Vanden Bosch promised to bring a specific bill of indictment to the next classical meeting, but he never did so. His charges were broadcast widely, however. He complained that the formula of subscription "was not binding, that people could not lodge protests, that many Freemasons were in the church, that the people had held a Prayer-day against the devilish spirit of suspicion of all those who could not agree with the goings-on, that Dr. Van

---

37 Brinks, "Church History via Kalamazoo," 37.
38 *Classis Holland Minutes*, 240.

Holland Museum Collection,
Joint Archives of Holland

Noordeloos Christian Reformed Church

Raalte was a member of the Freemasons, and that Dr. [sic.] Klijn had been right to say: 'We have given the hand to the Assyrians, and begged bread from the Egyptians!'" The charge about Van Raalte belonging to the Freemasons was certainly false, and the matter of the form of subscription not being binding was an open question, but the other items had some basis in fact.

Vanden Bosch also disapproved of the use of hymns, and he was shocked that Holland Classis condoned the decision of Vander Meulen to open his pulpit in the Zeeland church to Dominie Hendrik Scholte of Pella, even though Scholte had been deposed in 1840 by the Christian Seceder denomination in the Netherlands. "Those who told me these things (and many other things of a similar nature)," Vanden Bosch continued, "were no schismatics, self-seekers or 'black pots,' from whom men did not have to fear being polluted, as some men tried to say, but older pious folk whom I respected as pillars in God's church." The pious folk Vanden Bosch had in

---

39 Vanden Bosch's statements are quoted in Beets, "Vanden Bosch," 183-192. The debate about Scholte hinged on whether he had been deposed by a "general

mind were leaders in the churches of Graafschap, Vriesland, and Grand Rapids.[39]

Vanden Bosch paid a high price for his secession; he lost many members of his Noordeloos congregation and cut himself off from every minister in Holland Classis. He also jeopardized his salary, because Van Raalte instructed the secretary of the RCA Board of Domestic Missions, Rev. John Garretson, "Please stop the payments of the Dom. Board to revd. [Vanden] Bosch." As Vanden Bosch wrote: "I only retained 18 or 19 full members, in the middle of the forests of America, but I would rather be a wood-chopper than be a minister with a guilty conscience in a ruined and unreformed Church."[40]

Grand Rapids and Rev. Hendrik G. Klijn

Klijn began his letter of withdrawal with a prayer for oneness in Christ and closed by commending himself to your "fraternal friendship, that no spirit of bitterness may reign in us and among us, for we are brethren." We were "together ministers of the secession" of 1834, he reminded them, who had separated in the conviction that "the Church, the Bride of Christ, is a garden enclosed, a well shut up, and a fountain sealed." The words "enclosed," "shut up," "sealed," capture the essence of the Seceder fortress mentality that gave rise to the later motto of the CRC: "In isolation is our strength." Klijn's concern, which he told to Van Raalte privately, was that the RCA had become "liberal."[41]

Klijn himself was suspect in the eyes of the pietists. Wouter Jongste, a Seceder laborer from Goedereede, Province of Zeeland, reported after hearing several of Klijn's sermons in Grand Rapids: "Klijn preaches rather

     assembly" of the Christian Seceded Church at the 1840 synod, since delegates from several provinces had boycotted the synod meeting. *Classis Holland Minutes*, 223-224. See also Herbert Brinks, "Voices from our Immigrant Past: Origins of the Christian Reformed Church," *The Banner*, 16 June 1978, 14-15.

40   Beets, "Vanden Bosch,"183-192; Van Raalte to Garretson, 16 April 1857, box 13, fldr. 16, Correspondence of the Board of Domestic Missions of the Reformed Church, Archives of the RCA, New Brunswick, N. J. (copy in A. C. Van Raalte Institute).

41   Vanden Bosch to the consistory of Zeeland, 14 March 1857, which held his ministerial credentials, and Klijn to the classis assembly meeting 8 April at Zeeland, 6 April 1857 *Classis Holland Minutes*, 240-241, 245.

42   After emigrating in 1850, Jongste first lived in Grand Rapids and Polkton, Michigan; by 1870 he had settled in Paterson, N. J. There he admitted to Den Bleyker, "I don't dare stay home from church, but I will not join it." Jongste's negative reports on Reformed churches in Michigan and New Jersey gave the appearance of widespread apostasy in the RCA, says Brinks. Jongste to Den

well, but he fails to emphasize the work of the Holy Spirit sufficiently."[42] Duim, who had heard Klijn preach earlier in Illinois, also doubted his sincerity, declared that he was "not steadfast in doctrine or practice." When Klijn recanted his secession after six months and returned to the RCA, Duim felt vindicated. Krabshuis, too, condemned Klijn for returning "like a dog to his vomit." He is "now more liberal than any of the others, and everyone has lost confidence in him. He is in a bad state of mind and has no peace."[43]

Graafschap

The lengthy letter of the Graafschap consistory to the classis, signed by consistory president J.F. Van Anrooij and clerk Henry Strabbing, was the only communique that brought specific charges: the RCA introduced eight hundred hymns in worship "contrary to the church order"; it practiced open Communion; it failed to teach the catechism and ignored family visiting; and "what grieves our hearts the most in all this is that there are members among you who regard our secession in the Netherlands as not strictly necessary, or (think that) it was untimely."[44] The Graafschap believers of 1834 had suffered more from the civil authorities in Bentheim than did their Dutch brethren, and they had a strong emotional attachment to the Seceder Church.

The Graafschap consistory also cited Rev. Isaac Wyckoff's promise in 1849 that, should any congregations become dissatisfied with the union,

Bleyker, 10 October 1856, Den Bleyker Papers, as cited in Brinks, "Church History via Kalamazoo," 37; Robert P. Swierenga, comp., *Dutch Emigrants to the United States, South Africa, South America, and Southeast Africa, 1835-1880: An Alphabetical Listing by Household Heads and Independent Persons* (Wilmington, Del.: Scholarly Resources, 1983), 126; Robert P. Swierenga, comp., *Dutch Households in U.S. Population Censuses, 1850, 1860, 1870: An Alphabetical Listing by Family Heads*, 3 vols. (Wilmington, Del.: Scholarly Resources, 1987), 2:506.

43 Brinks, "Church History via Kalamazoo," 38-39. Klijn served as second pastor of the First Chicago RCA from 1862 to 1868.

44 *Classis Holland Minutes*, 242. In 1847 the RCA General Synod authorized the publication of a new songbook with 788 hymns. At the October 1856 classis session, the Graafschap church objected to this hymnbook (ibid., 226-227). For a brief history of the Graafschap settlement, see H. Beuker, *Tubantiana: Church-State Conflicts in Graafschap Bentheim, Germany* (1897), trans. Albert Hyma and Mrs. Peter Slenk (Holland, Mich.: Historical Library Committee, Graafschaap CRC, 1986); English translation, Holland, Mich., 1986; Swenna Harger and Loren Lemmen, *The County of Bentheim and her Emigrants to America* (Holland, Mich.: privately printed, 1990); H.J. Brinks, "Germans in the Christian Reformed Church, 1857-1872," *Origins* 9, no. 2 (1991): 36-43.

Calvin College Archives

Polkton Christian Reformed Church

they were "at liberty" to walk away. Wyckoff had given this personal promise to help persuade the doubters, but it was not and could not be an official policy of the RCA to give congregations carte blanche to secede. Rev. Vanden Bosch of Noordeloos chaired many Graafschap consistory meetings, including those considering secession beginning in March 1856.

The Graafschap letter of secession did not mention the issue of Freemasonry, but the consistory two months earlier had expressed among themselves a deep concern about the presence of Freemasons in the RCA.[45]

Polkton

Polkton was an isolated settlement of Seceders from the province of Groningen who in 1849 settled half way between Grand Rapids and Grand Haven. The few families met informally for worship for several years under the leadership of elder Lukas Elbers, until Holland Classis founded the church in 1854 with twenty-one souls. The declaration of secession by the consistory of this church was signed by elders Lucas Elbers and J.H. Vander

---

45 The deliberations of the Graafschap consistory from March 1856 to secession in 1857 are detailed in Beets, "Christian Reformed Church in N.A.," 1:88-90.

Werp, and deacon Henry Vinkemulder. It stated simply, "We have betaken ourselves to the standpoint we had when we left the Netherlands, in order thus again to be in connection with the church of the Netherlands."

Note that Polkton considered their action a return to the 1834 church. "The reason is your denomination fraternizes with those who are in opposition to the doctrine of our fathers.... Since there are others who have told you the points item by item, it is not necessary for us (to do so)." They concluded: "In the hope that God, who alone is able to make a roaring sea calm and smooth, may also make your hearts calm and smooth that you will walk with us in the way of our fathers."[46] Unstated complaints that surfaced later were the practice of permanent elderships and the refusal to keep the festival days.[47]

Van Raalte's Condemnation of Secession

With secession a fact, the dissenters gloated. "Apparently the 'pope' in Holland has never won the field entirely," crowed Den Bleyker.[48] But the letters of secession "grieved" Van Raalte deeply. He responded on the floor of the classis to these "serious (and) unsubstantiated accusations, ... which are the fruit of a lust for schism already for a long time manifested by a few leaders." Joining the RCA in 1850 in no way abandoned the 1834 secession, he insisted, because the RCA, contrary to the Hervormde Kerk directorate of 1816, upheld the traditional principles of Dort and the standard form of subscription for ministers.

Van Raalte charged that "the whole affair (excepting a few leaders who fan the fire of distrust and suspicion), is a mixture of ignorance, sectarianism, and a trampling under foot of the brethren, of which the ministers of the Classis of Holland have been constantly for years the prey." Such "gross ignorance, and palpable slanders," Van Raalte concluded, is impossible to refute by reasonable arguments. In a voice dripping with sarcasm, Van Raalte wished those "who fancy that they can create a holier and purer

---

46 Loren Lemmen, "The Early Church at Polkton, Michigan," *Origins* 12, no. 2 (1994): 39-42; *Classis Holland Minutes*, 243.
47 Kromminga, *Christian Reformed Church*, 25. The shortage of good elders in the early colony was the rationale for the decision. The Polkton CRC never obtained a pastor, and after one year it ceased sending delegates to the CRC classis meetings. Several families returned to the RCA and the rest simply functioned as an independent house church for many years. Lemmen, "Early Church at Polkton," 40, 42.
48 Brinks, "Church History via Kalamazoo," 38.

church than the Dutch Reformed Church of this country . . . to put us to shame and to be a blessing to us by spiritual prosperity and an active fruit-bearing Christianity."[49]

One can sympathize with Van Raalte's frustration with the critics. His profound sense of gratitude to the RCA for its constant and generous financial help to the colony was not shared by all. He was dealing with a skittish people who had suffered much in the Netherlands from distant synods and religious elites. Some brought a separatist mentality to Michigan and wanted to be free of formal ties to any American denomination. And they were a people who lacked firsthand information about the RCA in the East and could barely speak or read English in order to become better informed. This made them more dependent on forceful leaders and susceptible to rumormongers.

But the people in the pew also understood from their experience in the Netherlands Reformed Church that the spirit and life of a church might be heterodox while the formal doctrines yet appeared orthodox. They had seen and heard enough since arriving in the United States to be uneasy about various practices in the RCA, which had become increasingly Americanized since cutting itself loose from the Classis of Amsterdam early in the War for Independence. Three of the four documents of secession pleaded with the classis to remain tied to the mother church in the Netherlands, rather than to accept union with the RCA. John Kromminga may well be correct in saying that the seceders of 1857 did not have a "schismatic *intent*"; they were "expressing the true character of the church in the colony."[50]

Krabshuis, Van Raalte's ex-elder, voiced the 1834 mentality among the 1857 seceders. "By the Lord's grace," he wrote,

> we were led out of the Reformed Church hierarchy in the Netherlands when it became known that after 1816 the church was no longer of God—and the movement out of that church had been acknowledged by both friend and foe as the work of God.... Yes, I was allowed to participate in that sweet and harmonious fellowship, and the remembrance of those days lingers as the taste of honey on my lips.

49 *Classis Holland Minutes*, 243-249 (quotes on 245, 248).
50 Kromminga, "What Happened in 1857," 115; Herbert J. Brinks, "Another Look at 1857: The Birth of the CRC," *Origins* 4, no. 1 (1986): 27-31.

Holland Museum Collection, Joint Archives of Holland

Abraham Krabshuis

Shamefully, though, both the leaders and followers spoiled that harmony. For when they made other gods and laws, the Lord was angry and his spirit left them. Argumentation and division took the place of unity and peace. Still a remnant has remained in the Netherlands to witness publicly for the truth, and that same spirit was evident here in 1857. It was a sin for us to unite with a people we did not know. Yes, from the beginning, the Lord who first led us in the Netherlands has also done memorable deeds among us here.[51]

The Infant CRC—1857-1880

Most people in the colony did not leave Holland Classis. Only 10 percent seceded in 1857, totaling 150 families, 250 communicant members, 750 souls. The Grand Rapids church had about 100 members (50 families); Graafschap, 113 members (almost its entire congregation); Vriesland, 15 or

[51] Quoted in Brinks, "Church History via Kalamazoo," 40.

16 members (9 families); and Noordeloos and Polkton, each about 20 members. Graafschap was unique in that two-thirds of its members hailed from across the Dutch border in Bentheim. The first classis of the new denomination met in Holland in May of 1857, chaired by H.G. Klijn.[52]

Kromminga distinguished four conceptions about the church among the immigrants that form a continuum from narrowest to broadest. At the narrowest is the idiosyncratic and arbitrary views of Smit and Haan, which did not reflect the attitudes of most 1857 Seceders. Less narrow is the view of Vanden Bosch, who held to the strict doctrinal standards and customs of Dort. More broadly, there were those like Jannes Vande Luyster of Zeeland, who insisted on strict Reformed practice in the RCA but were willing to put some issues, such as Freemasonry, in the category of serious but not fatal flaws. They would cut the RCA a little slack until it got its house in order. The broadest conception of the church within the colony was that of Van Raalte, Vander Meulen, and Bolks, who held a very positive view of the RCA. The key breakpoint between seceders and nonseceders, Kromminga concluded, lay between the second and third positions, those who believed that churches must uphold standards but were not sure how rigidly to apply them. The differences were a matter of degree, not of kind. "But time, patience, information, and diplomacy were not sufficient to hold them together."[53]

Kromminga's continuum broadly reflects the divisions in the Netherlands among the Seceders of 1834 described in chapter 1. Smit, Haan, and Vanden Bosch were Cocksians and took their stand with Dort. Van Raalte and associates represented the more liberal southern wing of the Afscheiding; they were willing to adapt Dort to modern circumstances. The same essential fault line that ran through the 1834 secession, Herbert Brinks has explained, divided the pioneer churches of western Michigan. The leaders of all five seceding churches in 1857 held to a stricter interpretation of the Dort Church Order than did Van Raalte and associates who remained with the RCA.[54]

---

[52] D.H. Kromminga, *Christian Reformed Tradition*, 120; Beets, *Christian Reformed Church*, 71-72; Coopersville Reformed Church, *Ninetieth Anniversary Historical Booklet and Directory, 1854-1944* (Coopersville, 1944), 1-2.

[53] D.H. Kromminga, *Christian Reformed Tradition*, 115-116.

[54] Brinks, "Another Look at 1857," 30-31.

Revs. Koene Vanden Bosch and Wilhelmus H. Van Leeuwen

The fledgling church, which to make a statement chose the name True
Dutch Reformed Church, was a weak reed for many years, with the
Graafschap congregation the firmest rock. Koene Vanden Bosch was the
only ordained minister among the five charter congregations, because Klijn
returned to the RCA after six months.[55] Chief elder Haan shifted loyalties
between the CRC, RCA, and being independent. The church in Grand
Rapids was plagued with instability. The second pastor, Wilhelmus H. Van
Leeuwen, left after four hard years, and his successor, Roelof Duiker,
transferred to the RCA four years later. Vanden Bosch at Noordeloos was
embroiled in a long conflict with Jan Rabbers, who wished to organize a
Zeeland "branch." Polkton disintegrated within a year, while Vriesland and
Grand Haven were weak sisters. Consistory squabbles in Grand Rapids
(1861), Zeeland (1864), Noordeloos (1870), and Niekerk (1876) became so
intense that classical assemblies had to unseat them. Fortunately, the
Holland congregation, established under the leadership of Elder Krabshuis
in 1865, was stable. Primarily through lay leadership, flawed as it was, the
struggling seceder church survived the rocky years.[56] No price was too high
to pay in the defense of orthodoxy for the *True* Dutch Reformed Church.[57]

At the first classical gathering of the True brothers in May 1857, the ten
or so delegates reaffirmed the three forms of unity as "binding upon us" and

55 On 27 August 1857 Klijn wrote his former congregation at Graafschap to urge
them to "be reunited" with the RCA, as the synod of the mother church in the
Netherlands also recommended. "I am convinced from the word of God that we
by our secession have made ourselves guilty of schism in the body of our Lord and
Saviour Jesus Christ.... I was your leader in that sinful course, and went astray in
good faith.... We have sinned against our church confession in breaking off the
communion of the saints, and (against) all church rule and order, in withdrawing
from denominational fellowship without ever uttering a protest (against what we
thought was wrong)." Klijn to the Seceded Church of Graafschap, Mich., 27
August 1857, translation by Albertus Pieters in the Joint Archives of Holland,
Western Theological Seminary Collection. Klijn's last point about Graafschap
not giving reasons for secession overlooks the detailed letter (dated 7 April 1857)
that the consistory sent Holland Classis, which specified six reasons (*Classis
Holland Minutes,* 241-243).
56 Brinks, "Germans in the Christian Reformed Church," 39; Beets, "Christian
Reformed Church in N.A.," 2: 125-133. Beets here recites the sad litany of fallen
leaders, lay and clerical, and gives credit to the people in the pew. "We are
amazed at the steadfastness to principles of the followers more than that of many
of the leaders themselves" (133).
57 The new body struggled for years to settle on a name. The sixth classis meeting,
in 1859, adopted the name Holland Reformed Church. In 1861 this was changed
to True Dutch Church, in 1864 to True Holland Reformed Church, in 1868 to

Graafschap Christian Reformed Church

Niekerk Christian
Reformed Church

sent a letter to the mother church in the Netherlands, the Christelijke Afgescheiden Gereformeerde Kerk (CGKN), seeking union. But tensions in this body, stemming from the Afscheiding itself, led the Dutch brothers, after considerable discussion, to refuse to take sides in the conflict in Michigan. "We cannot judge concerning the division in North America. Act cautiously and in accordance with God's Word."

The True brothers did not take this as the last word; in 1860 and again in 1863 they wrote the CGKN seeking recognition and received the same rejection. The CRC might have changed minds if their synod early on had sent personal delegates to the Dutch synod, such as Holland Classis did in 1866 when it delegated Van Raalte himself, who planned an extended visit.

True Dutch Reformed Church, and in 1880 to Holland Christian Reformed Church. The Graafschap congregation, primarily from Graafschap Bentheim, objected to the word Dutch. The Paterson (N.J.) congregation objected to the adjective "True." Ardent 1834 seceders desired the same name as their mother body, the Christian Seceder Church. Beets, "Christian Reformed Church in N.A.," 2:123-124.

Private collection of Elton J. Bruins

Local History Department, Grand Rapids Public Library

*Grand Rapids
First Christian
Reformed Church*

*Holland Central Avenue
Christian Reformed Church*

Van Raalte assured the delegates of his denomination's orthodoxy and desire for closer fellowship. The Seceders, by contrast, said Van Raalte, "all too strongly wished to perpetuate the Dutch situation." His visit was a resounding public relations triumph. Finally, in 1872, the CRC sent its first delegates to the old Gereformeerde Kerk; they were received courteously but with little enthusiasm. Only in 1879, when the issue of "secret societies" surfaced (see chapter 4), did the stance of the CGKN begin to change.[58]

Meanwhile, the scattered Seceder congregations in Michigan struggled on alone. Vanden Bosch was stretched to the limit by itinerating among six congregations; he could only bring the Word and sacraments sporadically. Travel by ox cart through the forests was most difficult. "In my journeys," Vanden Bosch recalled, "I was several times in mortal danger, because at that time there were as yet no established roads. Always I had an ax and a

58 Willem van't Spijker, "The Christian Reformed Church and the Christelijke Gereformeerde Kerken in Nederland," 365-369 (quotes 366, 368), in Peter De Klerk and Richard De Ridder, eds., *Perspectives on the Christian Reformed Church: Studies in Its History, Theology, and Ecumenicity* (Grand Rapids: Baker Book House, 1983); Beets, "Christian Reformed Church in N.A.," 2: 139-149.

shovel with me in the wagon, so that when a tree had fallen across the road, I could shovel dirt against both sides so that I could ride over it."[59]

The pressures of the work and also his strong temper and domineering personality caused Vanden Bosch many difficulties, especially in the Zeeland contingent of his Noordeloos congregation. The Zeeland brothers did not recognize his place there, so Vanden Bosch deposed them. But when the CRC classis in 1859 called this act "rash," Vanden Bosch resigned his presidency and stormed out of the meeting. Since he was the only cleric in the classis, he had great leverage. The Zeeland problem festered until 1864, when the classis in an emotional session released the Zeeland congregation and consistory from Vanden Bosch's control. The brother relented only after the Rev. Douwe Vander Werp, who had recently come to serve the Graafschap church, prayed fervently and the assembly sang Psalm 142:7 (which speaks of honoring God's name for his righteousness), during which the Lord "worked mightily with his Spirit" and effected a "hearty reconciliation."

Unfortunately, Vanden Bosch caused quarreling and unrest in every church he served. As Beets noted: "The secession ship was almost foundered on the rock of brother-quarreling. It went badly sometimes in those days, almost as badly as in the earliest years of the secession in the Netherlands. It is a wonder that the Lord held the cause together!"[60]

Indeed, at the February 1863 meeting of the classis, Vanden Bosch proposed that the CRC join with the Old School Presbyterian Church, but the classis rejected this for the reason that the Presbyterians also used hymns in worship. Then Rev. Schepers of the Associate Reformed Church, who regularly attended CRC classis meetings, urged the body to join with his denomination, but this too was rejected. The CRC would continue on its independent course.[61]

---

59 Henry Zwaanstra, *Reformed Thought and Experience in a New World: A Study of the Christian Reformed Church and its American Environment, 1890-1918* (Kampen: H.J. Kok, 1973), 6; "CRC Classis Minutes," 26; Beets, "Vanden Bosch," *Gereformeerde Amerikaan*, April 1902, 190-192,

60 Beets, "Vanden Bosch," 225-229. After Noordeloos, Vanden Bosch served the Grand Haven and First Chicago churches. Psalm 142:7 in the Dutch Psalter reads: "Al uw getrouwen roep ik saam, als Gij mij zo hebt welgedaan, zij zullen horen hoe ik sing uwe name en uwe rechtvaardiging," which translated reads, "All your faithful ones I call together, since you have blessed me so, They will hear how I have honored your name in righteousness."

61 "CRC Classis Minutes," 25.

At the very classis meeting that rejected merger, Rev. Wilhelmus H. Van Leeuwen presented his credentials as the recently arrived pastor of the First Grand Rapids CRC. His coming was providential because he brought leadership and a trained mind, although he could be tendentious and had a checkered past.[62] The next classis meeting, in July 1863, appointed him to instruct interested ministerial students in his parsonage. Van Leeuwen was thus a precursor of the Calvin Theological School faculty. That same classis changed the name of the denomination to the "True Holland Reformed Church" and appointed Van Leeuwen, at his suggestion, to write a letter to the mother church in the Netherlands seeking recognition and formal affiliation.

The classis also appointed Van Leeuwen, Vanden Bosch, and elder P. Heyboer to write a defense of the CRC against attacks by the Holland Classis of the RCA, with the aim of publishing the same in the local press. Van Leeuwen pushed classis on other matters—to found Christian elementary schools and to consider union with the True Reformed Protestant Dutch Church in the East. This body, which stemmed from a secession in 1822 from the Reformed Protestant Dutch Church (RCA), finally merged with the CRC in 1890.[63]

Rev. Douwe J. Vander Werp, the Van Raalte of the Christian Reformed Church

In 1864 Rev. Douwe Vander Werp came to Graafschap CRC as its first pastor after the 1857 secession, and he quickly became the dominant minister in the CRC. As Herbert Brinks has written: Vander Werp "offered the 1857 seceders in America their closest link to the 1834 secession in Holland.... He became, in effect, the Van Raalte of the Christian Reformed Church." Vander Werp, an intimate protégé of de Cock and an associate of

---

62 Van Leeuwen (1807-1882) had served three Seceder churches in the Netherlands before emigrating without a call in 1856. First Reformed Church of Chicago hired him temporarily for six months, and he then took a call in 1857 to pastor the Holland (later Cedar Grove), Wisconsin, congregation, following Rev. Vander Schuur. In May 1859 Wisconsin Classis suspended him for committing the sin of adultery. See *Yearbook 1995 of the Christian Reformed Church*, 437; *Historical Directory of the Reformed Church in America, 1628-1978* (Grand Rapids: Wm. B. Eerdmans, 1978), 262; Wisconsin Classis Minutes, 18 May 1859, Joint Archives of Holland.
63 "CRC Classis Minutes," 22 July 1863 and 3 February 1864, 26-27, 33; Kromminga, *Christian Reformed Church*, 109-110, 200-201.

Calvin College Archives, l. and r.

Douwe J. Vander Werp   *Wilhelmus H. Van Leeuwen*

his son Helenius, was steeped in the Dortian orthodoxy of the northern wing of the Secession. The denomination tapped his strengths, appointing him to train students in his parsonage [which work after twelve years evolved into the Theological School (1876)], and naming him editor of the new denominational weekly, *De Wachter* (1868). Vander Werp was also delegated to organize new congregations at South Holland and Ridott (Ill.), Sheboygan, (Wis.), and Pella (Iowa); and to bring the Cincinnati (Ohio) congregation from the Scotch Presbyterians into the CRC. Closer to home he smoothed the way for Graafschap to mother the Holland (1865), Niekerk (1866), and East Saugatuck (1869) churches, and he resolved the long-standing dispute between Vanden Bosch and the Zeeland congregation. Like Van Leeuwen, Vander Werp was a strong advocate of Christian day schools and he opened a "Dutch school" in the summer months to teach children the mother tongue.[64]

---

[64] Brinks, "Germans in the Christian Reformed Church 1857-1872" 39-43, (quote 41).

Western Seminary Collection,
Joint Archives of Holland

Second Parsonage, Graafschap Christian Reformed Church

Christian Reformed Church Growth Rates

In the thirty years from 1873 to 1900, the Christian Reformed Church grew 800-fold, compared to a 100-fold increase in the immigrant congregations of the Reformed Church in America (table 1.1). By 1880 the younger denomination had 12,300 baptized and communicant members, compared to 112,000 in the senior denomination, of whom about 26,000 were immigrants.[65]

The CRC always appealed to immigrants who wished to preserve their Dutchness. It captured the bulk of the big immigrant wave of the 1880s, which mainly came from the northern provinces where de Cock and van Velzen had reigned supreme. These newcomers also brought with them the strong recommendation of the Gereformeerde Kerk to join the CRC because the RCA General Synod condoned lodge membership. That the two western classes of the RCA did not accept lodge members had little ameliorating effect in the GKN (see chapter 4).

[65] The estimated number of immigrant members (including baptized noncommunicants) in the RCA in 1880 by classis is: Albany 300, Holland 5,300, Geneva 2,000, Grand River 5,000, Illinois 6,000, Paramus 1,100, and Passaic 2,300 (*Acts and Proceedings of the General Synod of the Reformed Church in America,...* 1880).

Who Seceded in 1857 and Why?

Historians' views

A most interesting research question is to determine which people joined the CRC. Scholars have suggested several common socioeconomic characteristics of the 1857 seceders. The Netherlands historian Jacob van Hinte, who wrote the first scholarly history of the Dutch in America (1928), contended that many had not been part of the initial 1846-1847 contingent which had endured hardship together and learned to appreciate help from their Dutch-American brethren in the East.[66]

Van Hinte is undoubtedly correct. Only about one-quarter (52, or 22 percent) of the 242 known charter members of the Christian Reformed Church can be found among the 1846-1847 group of colonists. Another quarter (64, or 26 percent) emigrated in 1848 and 1849. However, the fact that the colony's population increased from 1,700 in 1847 to 6,000 in 1857 indicates that many settlers in 1857, not just the dissenters, lacked the experience of the early struggles.

A more complex theory is that of Henry Beets, the first historian of the Christian Reformed Church. Beets reported, "It was said in the Netherlands at the time that Groningers went to the seceders [Christian Reformed Church] while the Frisians, Zeelanders, Overiselers, and Hollanders [Noord- and Zuid-Holland] went to the Reformed Church."[67]

Van Hinte adds a variation to this provincial scheme by insisting that the seceders of 1857 were, in the main, members of the rural and conservative northern party in the Netherlands, whereas the more broadminded southern party of Van Raalte remained with the Reformed Church in the East. Van Eyck agrees that the southern party dominated the Holland colony until the 1880s immigration gave the northern party its strength. Van Hinte also adds a class distinction—the Christian Reformed founders were poorer and lived mainly in the big city of Grand Rapids.[68]

---

[66] Jacob van Hinte, *Netherlanders in America: A Study of Emigration and Settlement in the Nineteenth and Twentieth Centuries in the United States of America* (1928),ed. Robert P. Swierenga, trans. Adriaan de Wit (Grand Rapids: Baker Book House, 1985), 360-366; Henry Ryskamp, "The Dutch in Western Michigan" (Ph.D. diss., University of Michigan, Ann Arbor, 1936), 29-30.

[67] Quoted in Ryskamp, "Dutch in Western Michigan," 32. The time period that Beets had in mind is not stated, but he may have intended the years after 1880.

[68] Van Hinte, *Netherlanders in America,* 381-382.

This latter point was disputed by sociologist Henry Ryskamp, who contended that over half of the seceding families in the Grand Rapids area lived outside the city, and that the "urban-rural distribution of the Reformed Church, if not at that time, after 1857 was about the same as that of the Seceding Church."[69] All the scholars agree that the genesis of the 1857 split was in the divisions among the seceders of 1834 in the Netherlands, particularly that between the southern wing of Brummelkamp and the northern wing of de Cock and van Velzen.

Background of RCA and CRC members

This issue can be clarified by comparing American church membership lists with the Dutch emigration lists, which tell for each family the place of last residence, occupation, social class, denominational affiliation, and year of departure.[70]

By comparing church records[71] against emigration lists, I have assembled a background profile of 2,180 Dutch immigrant family heads and single adults in the years before 1880. Of these immigrants, 1,151 belonged to immigrant congregations of the RCA and 1,029 were affiliated with the CRC. This is a sufficient sample for a comparative analysis of the membership of the two denominations, although it is not without some deficiencies, because Dutch emigration lists are incomplete before 1848. Since the 1857 secession is the key event in the history of the Reformed churches in America, I will focus especially on this seminal period. The pre-1857 group totals 973 heads of households and single adults, 731 in the RCA and 242 in the CRC.

69 Ryskamp, "Dutch in Western Michigan," 29.
70 Swierenga, *Dutch Emigrants to the United States*. This analysis is taken from my paper, "Local-Cosmopolitan Theory and Immigrant Religion: The Social Bases of the Antebellum Dutch Reformed Schism," *Journal of Social History* 14 (fall 1980): 113-35. Unfortunately, emigration lists are not extant for 779 emigrant families and single adults in the years 1831-1847. In the key years of the congregational migration, 1845-1847, 21 percent of the emigrant lists are not extant. This fact must always be kept in mind when interpreting the available records. Van Raalte's entire Velp-Arnhem congregation of 1834 Seceders, for example, is not included in the Dutch Emigration records in this study sample. The Seceder impact on the Reformed Church in America is thus underestimated.
71 Church membership lists were compiled from church anniversary booklets, membership lists, baptism records, and consistory minutes, which are available in Calvin College Archives; Joint Archives of Holland; Herrick Public Library, Holland, Mich.; and Archives of the RCA. Church membership lists are extant for fewer than a dozen congregations prior to 1870.

The major questions are: Were the seceders of 1857 any different than the nonseceders? Did they have different religious, social, and economic backgrounds in the old country? And if so, which background characteristics are significant and which are not, in distinguishing between the two groups?

The results are as follows. First, and most amazingly, there is no direct correlation between the seceders of 1834 and those of 1857 (table 3.2). One-third (148) of the 395 seceders of 1834 living in Michigan before 1857 seceded again in 1857, and they went in *equal proportions* (about 45 percent) into the RCA and CRC.[72] Surprisingly, the other 55 percent of members in both denominations were of Hervormde Kerk background, which means that Hervormden comprised the majority in both denominations.[73] A possible explanation for the large number of Hervormde Kerk immigrants joining the CRC is that they were secret sympathizers of the Christian Seceded Church who lacked the courage or opportunity to join themselves. Many also may have chosen the CRC because it was less Americanized. We need to know much more about these Hervormde immigrants, who are overlooked by historians.

Second, the CRC and RCA people in Michigan had virtually the same socioeconomic background (table 3.3). Local government officials in the Netherlands classified each departing family economically into three categories: well-to-do, middling, and needy. The RCA had a slightly larger proportion of wealthy immigrants, but it also included more poor families. The charter members of the CRC had comparatively more families of middling origin. Occupationally, more than 90 percent in both groups

72 Given the prominent place of 1834 seceders in the denominational literature of the American Reformed churches, these figures showing the low incidence of seceder origin are quite unexpected. Historians have not given the immigrants of Hervormde Kerk background as much attention as they deserve. Elton J. Bruins, *The Americanization of a Congregation: A History of the Third Reformed Church of Holland, Michigan*, rev. ed. (Grand Rapids: Wm. B. Eerdmans, 1995); Hyma, *Van Raalte*; Irene and John A. Dykstra, *A History of Central Reformed Church, Grand Rapids, Michigan: It Is Yet Building* (n.p., 1968); Bruins, "Immigration," in *Piety and Patriotism: Bicentennial Studies of the Reformed Church in America, 1776-1976*, ed. James W. Van Hoeven (Grand Rapids: Wm. B. Eerdmans, 1976), 56-76.
73 Comparable figures for immigrants of Hervormde Kerk origin in the post-schism period 1858-1880 are 80 percent and 61 percent, respectively, in the Reformed and Christian Reformed denominations. This indicates that the post-1857 pattern is substantially different.

worked with their hands, but the CRC included a slightly higher proportion of farmers and day laborers and fewer white collar people than did the RCA (table 3.4). Finally, in age and family characteristics, heads of immigrant households in both denominations were virtually identical.[74]

Of all the behavioral characteristics, the only discriminating factor I could find appears to be place of origin. This, of course, is a proxy for historic cultural and religious differences. As table 3.5 and figure 3.1 show, the CRC members came mainly from Groningen, Drenthe, Overijssel, and Zeeland. RCA families, by contrast, came largely from Noord- and Zuid-Holland, Utrecht, Gelderland, and Friesland.

Within the provinces there were differences by subregion. In Zeeland, for example, which is composed of three groups of island "fingers" in the Rhine delta, immigrants from the islands closest to Rotterdam (Schouwen-Duiveland-Tholen) were more likely by two to one to join the Christian Reformed Church. Among those from the middle island group of Walcheren-Zuid Beveland, the ratio was nearly one for one. But among immigrants from Zeeuws-Vlaanderen along the Belgian border, the RCA attracted six families for every four who joined the CRC.

Immigrants from Groningen who joined the CRC were concentrated in the northernmost region, particularly the municipalities of Ulrum and Leens, where Hendrik de Cock's influence was so strong. De Cock trained many of the young men who went to America after the Civil War to pastor Christian Reformed congregations. Similarly, in Gelderland, which comprises three distinct regions—the Achterhoek, Veluwe, and Betuwe—the conservative Veluwe area near the Zuiderzee and the very similar neighboring province of Overijssel provided more members for the Christian Reformed Church than did the more liberal Achterhoek area on the German border and the more urban Betuwe region that lay astride the Rhine and includes the cities of Arnhem and Nijmegen.

In the twenty-five years after 1857, there is a marked shift northward in the regional origins of CRC members; nearly one-half of the CRC members originated in the northern provinces of Drenthe, Friesland, and Groningen,

---

74 Both averaged 38 years at the time of resettlement and the number of children per family was 3.6 for those affiliating with the Reformed Church and 3.5 for those joining the 1857 Seceder Church. The respective percentages of immigrant "units" or households with a mate was 65 and 72, the percentage of units with children was 61 and 66, and the percentage of male-headed units was 96 and 98.

whereas before 1857 less than one-third did so (table 3.5). If the rural eastern regions of Overijssel and the Veluwe of Gelderland are added, the northern Netherlands contingent in the CRC rises to two-thirds.

Among immigrant families in the RCA, there is also a northward shift after 1857, but the southern and western areas of the Netherlands furnished 40 percent of the members. Thus, the post-1857 migration from the northern Netherlands fixed the unique and enduring character of the Christian Reformed Church that had been presaged by the early immigration.

Background of CRC Ministers

The ministers who served the CRC mirrored even more clearly than the laity its northern seceder character. Of the 114 clerics ordained in the CRC from 1857 to 1900, every one had been affiliated with the Seceded denomination in the Netherlands, and three-quarters (88) originated in the northern provinces. Of the 132 clerics ordained in the midwestern classes of the RCA in the years 1846-1900, at least 116 were also Dutch-born, but of these only one-quarter (30) had been 1834 seceders and only 42 percent (49) were from the northern provinces. This was less than half as many as among the CRC ministers.[75] Thus, the different origins of the leaders were even more pronounced than those among the rank and file. And their honored status as *dominies* ("lords") gave them a special role in molding opinion in the community.

In sum, the members of the sister Dutch Reformed denominations in the last half of the nineteenth century had different social bases in the old country. The CRC clearly reflected the orthodox mentality of the northern Netherlands and the piety of those from northern Zeeland, while the RCA bore the more congenial marks of the Randstad and central heartland.[76]

---

[75] These figures are from a collective biographical study by Herbert J. Brinks, "Voices from Our Immigrant Past: Origins of the Christian Reformed Church," *The Banner,* 2 June 1978, 16-18. For a brilliant analysis of the connections between the Dutch and American churches, see Brinks, "Religious Continuities in Europe and the New World," 209-223; and Brinks, "The Christian Reformed Church and the Reformed Church in America: A Study of Comparative Cultural Adaptation in America," (paper presented to the Great Lakes History Conference, Grand Rapids, 1979).

[76] In a behavioral study of Americanization among evangelical and conservative clerical factions in the Dutch and German Reformed churches in late colonial America, Johannes Jacob Mol concluded that different theological orientations rather than behavioral factors accounted for varying rates of assimilation. It is argued here, however, that localism or cosmopolitanism is a surrogate for such

Conclusion

This finding may explain why members of the midwestern RCA were more willing to accommodate themselves theologically, ecclesiastically, and culturally to their new environment, whereas the CRC continued to look to the mother country for leadership and direction.[77] The RCA members acted like immigrants and CRC members acted like colonists. The CRC desired a transplanted community, a little Holland, where they could continue life as they had known and valued it, but with a higher living standard. The CRC remained an immigrant church until after the First World War, and became, in the words of Yale history professor Sidney Ahlstrom, "The country's most solid and dignified bastion of conservative Reformed doctrine and church discipline."[78]

theological and religious differences. See Mol, "Theology and Americanization: The Effects of Pietism and Orthodoxy on Adjustment to a New Culture" (Ph.D. diss., Columbia University, 1960).

[77] See Brinks, "Voices from our Immigrant Past"; and Paul Honigscheim, "Religion and Assimilation of the Dutch in Michigan," *Michigan Historical Magazine* 26 (winter 1942): 54-66.

[78] Sydney E. Ahlstrom, *A Religious History of the American People* (New Haven: Yale University Press, 1972), 755.

Table 3.1: *Reformed and Christian Reformed Church Growth Rates, 1873-1899 (in percent)*

Denomination	1873-1875	1875-1881	1881-1884	1884-1887	1887-1890	1890-1893	1893-1896	1896-1899
Reformed°								
Periodic rate	3	4	3	6	2	10	7	4
Cumulative rate	3	7	10	17	19	31	40	45
Reformed (immigrant classes only)#								
Periodic rate	18	3	3	20	14	14	6	2
Cumulative rate	18	22	25	50	70	94	106	111
Christian Reformed+								
Periodic rate	41	52	66	31	28	28	11	9
Cumulative rate	41	116	257	367	496	664	748	831

° Based on number of families, communicant and noncommunicant.

\# Includes Wisconsin, Grand River, Holland, Illinois, Iowa, and Dakota classes.

+ Based on number of souls, communicants and baptized members, including children.

Sources: *The Acts and Proceedings of the General Synod of the Reformed Church in America*, 1873-1899; *Christian Reformed Church Jaarboeken*, 1875, 1881-1899; *De Wachter*, 19 September 1973.

Table 3.2: *Netherlands and U.S. Denominational Affiliation Compared, Pre- and Post-1857 Immigrants, Household Heads and Single Persons*

| Netherlands Affiliation | 1835-1856 | | | | 1857-1880 | | | |
| | Reformed | | Christian Reformed | | Reformed | | Christian Reformed | |
	N	%	N	%	N	%	N	%
Hervormde Kerk	383	54	214	55	341	80	388	61
1834 Seceder	321	45	171	44	84	20	242	38

Source: Robert P. Swierenga, comp., *Dutch Emigrants to the United States, South Africa, South America, and Southeast Asia, 1835-1880: An Alphabetical Listing by Household Heads and Independent Persons* ((Wilmington, Del.: Scholarly Resources, 1983); augmented for the years 1831-1847 with data from the Department of Binnenlandsche Zaken report in "Staat van landverhuizers 1831-1847," *Nederlandsche Staatscourant*, 5 September 1848, 2. Church membership lists were compiled from church anniversary booklets, membership lists, baptism records, and consistory minutes which are available at Calvin College Archives, Grand Rapids, Mich.; Joint Archives of Holland, Holland, Mich.; Herrick Public Library, Holland, Mich.; and Archives of the RCA, New Brunswick, N.J. Church membership lists are extant for fewer than a dozen congregations prior to 1870.

Table 3.3: *Netherlands Social Classes by U.S. Denominational Affiliation, Pre- and Post-1857 Immigrants, Household Heads and Single Persons*

| Socioeconomic Classes | 1835-1856 | | | | 1857-1880 | | | |
| | Reformed | | Christian Reformed | | Reformed | | Christian Reformed | |
	N	%	N	%	N	%	N	%
Well-to-do	98	16	47	13	57	13	45	7
Middling	401	64	253	68	303	70	472	74
Poor	125	20	70	19	71	16	120	19

Table 3.4: *Netherlands Occupational Classification by U.S. Denominational Affiliation, Pre- and Post-1857 Immigrants, Household Heads and Single Persons*

Occupational Classification	1835-1856				1857-1880			
	Reformed		Christian Reformed		Reformed		Christian Reformed	
	N	%	N	%	N	%	N	%
White Collar/ Professional	51	8	18	5	21	5	35	6
Owners	147	23	95	26	73	17	83	13
Skilled Workers	147	27	85	23	87	21	106	17
Unskilled & Farm Laborers	277	43	170	46	240	57	397	64

Table 3.5: *Netherlands Province of Last Residence by U.S. Denominational Affiliation, Pre- and Post-1857 Immigrants, Household Heads and Single Persons, 1835-1880*

Province	1835-1856				1857-1880			
	Reformed		Christian Reformed		Reformed		Christian Reformed	
	N	%	N	%	N	%	N	%
Drenthe	35	5	32	13	6	1	5	7
Friesland	68	9	16	7	31	7	83	11
Gelderland	124	17	18	7	99	24	92	12
Groningen	82	11	28	12	103	24	222	28
Noord-Brabant	8	1	4	2	7	2	13	2
Noord-Holland	32	4	5	2	31	7	40	5
Overijssel	76	10	47	19	18	4	44	6
Utrecht	17	2	2	1	4	1	5	1
Zeeland	177	24	67	28	59	14	112	14
Zuid-Holland	112	15	23	10	62	15	118	15
Totals	731	100%	242	100%	420	100%	787	100%

Figure 3.1: *The Provincial Divisions of the Netherlands Showing Primary Regions of Origins of Immigrant Members of the Christian Reformed and Reformed Churches in America, 1835-1880.*

IV
1882
Secession Yet Again:
The Masonic Controversy

The Reformed Church in America endured a series of controversies and subsequent secessions related to the question of adaptation to the American culture and society. The Coetus-Conferentie controversy in the 1740s, as explained in chapter 1, was a debate about the formation of an American classis which would give the Dutch Reformed churches an ecclesiastical organization of their own. The "American" party argued that an American classis would enable the RCA to conduct some of its own affairs—the most crucial being the right to ordain its own candidates for the ministry—without having to get permission from the Amsterdam Classis in the Netherlands every time it wanted to act.

The Americanization issue was not settled for the midwestern Dutch immigrant churches with the Secession of 1857 and the formation of the CRC. The majority of the Dutch immigrant churches that stemmed from the 1847 immigration to the Middle West under the direction of Van Raalte in Michigan and Scholte in Iowa remained with the RCA. The founders of the CRC, who were opposed to the Union of 1850, were not joined by many other Dutch immigrants during the 1857-1880 period. The majority of the Dutch immigrant congregations in Michigan, Illinois, Wisconsin, and Iowa simply learned to live with sister congregations in New York and New Jersey, many of which had over the course of 250 years fully adapted to the American religious and cultural scene.

For various reasons, the union between the old Dutch immigrants in the East and the new Dutch immigrants of the Middle West was never completely satisfactory. Under the leadership of Van Raalte, however, the interests of the two groups were melded, and Van Raalte was able to channel gifts and monies from the eastern churches to aid the new immigrant congregations. Eastern money helped to establish in Holland, Michigan, the Pioneer School in 1851, the Pillar church in 1856, and Hope College in 1866. Scholte never united with the Reformed Church, but most of his followers did so. Moreover, the RCA churches of the East and West joined in efforts to evangelize the world during the period of growing interest in foreign missions which swept the American churches in the nineteenth century.

However, the community of interests between the eastern and western churches of the RCA between 1868 and 1880 was severely jarred by an unusually difficult dispute concerning membership in secret societies, the lodge of the Freemasons in particular. Although Calvinist churches in Europe and North America were opposed to Freemasonry in general, the RCA in New York and New Jersey had, during its process of Americanization in the eighteenth century, accepted the lodge as part of American society, and many of its members joined the lodge as a matter of course. The new Dutch immigrants of the nineteenth century, fresh from the Netherlands, were unanimous in the opinion that Freemasonry was an anti-Christian organization and that membership in the lodge or in any secret society should be forbidden. The western churches believed, further, that members of churches who were Freemasons should be disciplined and expelled if they did not resign their lodge membership. The issue proved so divisive and so difficult to settle that a new secession from the RCA resulted in 1882. The impact of this secession was equal to that of 1822 and greater than that of the Secession of 1857.

To understand the issues that led to the Secession of 1882, it is necessary to understand the nature of Freemasonry and the reasons why the mainstream

American Protestant churches, including the RCA, were able to accept lodge membership as a support of Christianity and not as an opponent. Freemasonry was founded in England in 1717.[1] It derived from the masons' guilds which had existed for centuries and which had built the cathedrals of Europe. However, beginning in 1717, the guilds developed into lodges which accepted members interested in history, philosophy, and science as well, and the lodges became speculative organizations rather than operative ones. To be an "accepted" mason, one did not have to be a working mason. Instead, the guild became a fraternal and social organization with its own myth, symbolism, and ritual along speculative lines. Actually, the lodge was a child of the Enlightenment. The lodge of Freemasons affirmed a religious and moral universalism and had a universally shared apprehension of evil.[2]

Freemasonry spread rapidly into Europe and to North America. The first lodge in the Netherlands was founded in 1725 at the Hague, although the Calvinist clergy were hostile to it, and forty-six more lodges had been established by 1871. Because of England's ties with North America, the lodge was immediately exported to the American colonies. As a young man, Benjamin Franklin joined the lodge in 1731. By 1800, many thousands of men in North America had become Masons, and Freemasonry and other lodges had become a vital part of the American social structure and a recognized part of society. According to Dorothy Lipson, the lodge "offered

---

[1] For general background on Freemasonry in Europe and the United States of America, see Dorothy Ann Lipson, *Freemasonry in Federalist Connecticut* (Princeton: Princeton University Press, 1977); J. Fletcher Brennan, *A General History of Freemasonry* (Cincinnati: American Masonic Publishing Association, 1871); Elijah Alfred Coil, *The Relation of the Liberal Churches and the Fraternal Orders* (Boston: American Unitarian Association, 1927); David B. Davis, "Some Themes of Counter-Subversion: An Analysis of Anti-Masonic, Anti-Catholic, and Anti-Mormon Literature," *Mississippi Valley Historical Review* 47 (1960/61): 205-224; James Dewar, *The Unlocked Secret: Freemasonry Examined* (London: William Kimber, 1966); Charles Grandison Finney, *The Character, Claims and Practical Workings of Freemasonry* (Chicago: National Christian Association, 1913); Walton Hannah, *Darkness Visible: A Revelation and Interpretation of Freemasonry* (London: Augustine Press, 1952); Melvin M. Johnson, *The Beginnings of Freemasonry in America* (New York: George H. Doran Co., 1924); Gerard M. Van Pernis, *Masonry, Antithesis of the Christ* (Grand Rapids: Wm. B. Eerdmans, 1932); Nesta Helen Webster, *Secret Societies and Subversive Movements* (London: Boswell Printing and Publishing Co., 1928); and William Joseph Whalen, *Christianity and American Freemasonry* (Milwaukee: Bruce Publishing Co., 1958).

[2] Lipson, *Freemasonry in Federalist Connecticut*, chapter 1.

the many pleasures of fraternal conviviality." Nor was the lodge seen as inimical to the interests of American Christianity, although in the case of men like Franklin, who were not church members, the lodge fulfilled a religious function.[3]

Since the lodge was seen primarily as a fraternal and social organization, many men who were Christians joined the lodges and personally experienced no conflicts between lodge values and ideas and their Christian beliefs and value systems. In time, the clergy even gave its blessing to fraternal organizations such as Freemasonry. For instance, Ashbel Baldwin, a Congregational clergyman, became the chaplain of the Connecticut Grand Lodge in 1797. A son of Jonathan Edwards, the great theologian of the eighteenth century, also served as a grand master of the Connecticut lodge. The Universalist clergy were the first to join the lodges in Connecticut, but when Congregationalist clergy also joined, people concluded that men in good standing in their churches could join the lodges in good conscience. For Christians, the "Great Light" or source of truth in Masonry was the Bible, and the Bible was considered the basis for Masonic myth and ritual. One thing the clergymen affiliated with lodges insisted on was that the morality which Masonry affirmed was the morality which Christianity had affirmed. By 1800, Freemasonry was for the most part a widely accepted institution in North America, highly regarded by many and, according to Masons, not considered to conflict with basic Christianity.[4]

Masonry's wide acceptance in North America, however, does not mean that it did not engender opposition. There has always been in American society an undercurrent of opposition to secret societies on both theological and social grounds. Outsiders perceived the secrecy of the lodge as threatening. There was also an inherent elitism in lodge membership; men of the higher social and economic class were more likely to be members of lodges than those from the lower class. But opposition grew for religious reasons, too. The orthodox clergymen in Connecticut, for instance, believed that Masonry was at odds with Calvinism and held that some members used the lodge as a surrogate religion. Such clerics refused to accept Masons into

---

3 Brennan, *General History of Freemasonry*, 123; David Freeman Hawke, *Franklin* (New York: Harper and Row, 1976), 44; and Lipson, *Freemasonry in Federalist Connecticut*, 9.

4 Lipson, *Freemasonry in Federalist Connecticut*, 92-93, 129.

the church. For similar theological reasons, the Roman Catholic Church had banned the Masonic order in Europe shortly after its formation in 1717.[5]

The first major outburst of opposition to Freemasonry in North America occurred in 1826 as a reaction to the abduction and presumed murder of William Morgan of western New York.[6] A former Mason, Morgan announced an exposé of Freemasonry and disappeared soon after. He was never seen alive again and his body was never found. His abductors were members of the Freemasons, but they received only very light sentences from a jury composed of Masons. The scandalous affair crystallized the opposition to Masonry, and by 1828 a formal anti-Masonry movement, combining an evangelical impulse with political action, had been organized. The movement became a political party, and many anti-Masonic publications sprang up. The movement was active for about five years.

The RCA in New York and New Jersey paid no formal attention to anti-Masonry. A committee of the General Synod reported annually that it deplored the decline of the Sabbath in American life and the rise of intemperance, but there is no evidence in the minutes of the General Synod or particular synods that there was any sympathy with the anti-Masonic movement in the later part of the 1820s.[7] At the same time, the dissident True Reformed Protestant Dutch Church, which had originated in the Secession of 1822 went on record very clearly in response to the Morgan affair. Masonry was to be condemned, and membership in the lodge was not to be permitted among members of the denomination.[8] Since this new

---

5 Ibid., 9, 120, 127-132. In 1738 Pope Benedict XIV renewed the bull of excommunication that Clement XII had issued against the Freemasons. Brennan, *General History of Freemasonry*, 320.

6 Lipson, *Freemasonry in Federalist Connecticut*, 267-273, gives a thorough account of this event.

7 Article XVII, entitled, "Prevailing Sins," in *The Acts and Proceedings of the General Synod of the Reformed Dutch Church in North America,...June, 1829.* Freemasonry was never mentioned, nor was it alluded to in the synodical reports on the state of the church.

8 A full account of their action is worth noting: "The Committee on the subject of Freemasonry ask leave to report——Your Committee are aware, that the Masonic Institutions and Principles have lately attracted much public attention in this country; several pamphlets and books on the subject, have been published, professing to reveal the nature and tendency of its secrets. Among these publications, 'Bernard's Light on Masonry,' holds a conspicuous place. The members of the masonic fraternity appear to be numerous in every part of the

denomination was clearly opposed to the RCA, from which it had seceded, this action can also be interpreted as a reaction to the RCA, which had not condemned Masonry and had remained silent about the scandalous Morgan affair.

Given the magnitude of the opposition to Masonry, the failure of the RCA to mention Morgan's murder at the synodical level suggests that it had already become Americanized to the extent that it could not publicly condemn membership in an organization which many of its members had joined.[9] When the question of membership in the lodge did reach the General Synod of the RCA in 1868, the attitude of the eastern churches toward the lodge prevailed: the lodge was not viewed as anti-Christian but compatible with Christianity, and membership in the lodge was left to individual consciences.

The issue of Freemasonry had not been mentioned when the Dutch immigrant churches in Michigan united with the RCA in 1850. The newcomers shared the attitude generally held in the Netherlands that membership in the lodge was a sin and they assumed that the RCA was of the same mind. Van Raalte had rightly assured his people that the old RCA in the East was not influenced by the liberalism which plagued the Hervormde Kerk in the Netherlands and that the piety of the churches in the East was very similar to that of the colonists in Holland.

United States; belonging to every class in society, whether civil or religious, and some of the highest standing. As to the civil, or political character of the institution, we deem it not necessary, at present, to make any remarks; but as to the religious nature and pretensions of this mysterious association, as far as revealed, we think it demands the attention of the Synod. The Masonic Society professes to find its foundation in the sacred volume;—to have an intimate relation with Solomon's Temple; and to be a religious fraternity—a household of faith—a band of mystic brethren. Examining it in this light, we find the religion of the Association to be a mixture of Paganism and Mohammedanism, with the corruptions of Judaism and Christianity; for many professed Christians, many Papists, Jews, and even Gentiles, are found in its communion. We also find, that it perverts the meaning and use of the Bible, is full of names of blasphemy, and administers illegal, profane, and horrible oaths. We are decidedly of this opinion, that no true Christian can, consistently with his profession, to be a free and accepted mason—and that the ministers and members of our true Reformed Dutch Church can have no fellowship with this fraternity." *Acts and Proceedings of the General Synod of the True Reformed Dutch Church in the United States of America,...June, 1831*, 10-11.

9 Peter Hoekstra, "The American Revolt against Freemasonry," *Reformed Journal* 9 (April 1959):20, incorrectly credited the Dutch Reformed Church (RCA) with this action.

But as the old RCA in the East and the new RCA in the West came to know each other better, differences due to the Americanization process in the East began to appear. One of them was the attitude toward the lodge. The first mention of the lodge issue was made in the Classis of Holland in 1853. The classis made quick work of the issue and said that because Masonry was among the works of darkness it was "thus unlawful for a [church] member" to belong to a Masonic lodge.[10] There were no lengthy debates, no majority and minority opinions, and no reference to the attitude on Freemasonry in the denomination. This was a local matter, and the Classis of Holland expressed the traditional European and Dutch attitudes.

Henry Beets, an eminent historian of the CRC, claimed that Freemasonry was one of the formal causes for a group of people leaving the RCA in 1857 and organizing a new denomination for Dutch immigrants.[11] This was not the case, however. The formal reasons that gave rise to the secession were that hymns were acceptable for use in the RCA, that non-Reformed Protestants were accepted at the Lord's Supper in some RCA churches in the East, and that the preaching of the Heidelberg Catechism and regular family visitation by ministers and elders was falling into disuse.[12] Masonry was not listed in the complaint to the classes. Within a decade, however, the infant CRC took formal action against membership in the lodge.

The controversy about Masonry began in earnest in 1867, when the CRC officially banned membership in the lodge by synodical order, just as its sister, the True Reformed Protestant Dutch Church in the East, had done in 1831.[13] The midwestern immigrant churches of the RCA were not about to suffer by comparison with the CRC, so in 1868 the Classis of Wisconsin, under the leadership of John H. Karsten, Herman Stobbelaar, and Hendrik G. Klijn [Kleijn], sent a memorial to the General Synod of the RCA, asking it to declare that membership in the church and the lodge were incompatible and to condemn Masonry. The General Synod voted to take no action by a vote of eighty-nine to nineteen. Van Raalte, Jacob and John Vander Meulen

10 *Classis Holland Minutes 1848-1858* (Grand Rapids: Wm. B. Eerdmans, 1950), 144.
11 Henry Beets, *The Christian Reformed Church in North America, Its History, Schools, Missions, Creed and Liturgy, Distinctive Principles and Practices and its Church Government* (Grand Rapids: Eastern Avenue Book Store, 1923), 47.
12 *Classis Holland Minutes*, 242.
13 "Minutes of the Highest Assembly of the Christian Reformed Church, 1857-1880" (English translation, Calvin College Archives), 77.

(the sons of the founder of Zeeland, Michigan, Cornelius Vander Meulen), and Karsten all voted with the small minority.[14]

The midwestern Dutch immigrant churches soon confirmed their representatives' opposition to the General Synod's ruling. In 1869 the classes of Holland and Wisconsin went to the General Synod with overtures reaffirming their position of 1868, but the synod referred the matter to a committee for further consideration.[15] In 1870, the General Synod made itself very clear on the issue: membership in a secret society, they declared, was not a good practice; church members should not belong. This statement was clearly a concession to the protesters from the West. But many members of the General Synod were undoubtedly Masons, and the synod declared further that it could not and would not rule that membership in the lodge was to be forbidden by church law. In explaining its thinking, the General Synod maintained that if it had disallowed membership in the lodge, it would have set up a new test of membership and, moreover, it would have interfered with consistorial privileges. Only the local consistory admitted new members, and it alone had the prerogative to decide who could be a member of the church and who could not.[16] The General Synod has never budged from this position, leaving it to the consistory to declare whether membership in the lodge was compatible or incompatible with membership in the local church.

Most of the Dutch immigrant churches in the Middle West accepted this ruling, and consistories continued to ban Masons from church membership as they would have done had they still been in the Netherlands. Even though Van Raalte voted against the action of the synod in 1868, he later declared that membership in the lodge was a matter for discipline only if the church

---

[14] *Acts and Proceedings of the General Synod of the Reformed Church in America,...1868*, 463.

[15] *Acts and Proceedings of the General Synod of the Reformed Church in America,...1869*, 662.

[16] The minute reads as follows: "Our brethren are evidently sincere and earnest in their convictions. They are greatly perplexed on account of what they perceive to be a serious evil in the Church, and they have done well to state their difficulties. We cannot think, however, that they expect from Synod such a deliverance as would authorize Consistories to exclude Free Masons from church fellowship, for this would be to establish a new and unauthorized test of membership in the Christian Church, and would interfere with consistorial prerogatives" (*Acts and Proceedings of the General Synod of the Reformed Church in America,...1870*, 96-97).

members lived in such a manner as to give cause for disciplinary action.[17] Clearly, Van Raalte had Americanized in his attitude toward Freemasonry. He did not like the Freemasons and would never have joined the lodge himself, but after 1868 he no longer voiced the traditional Dutch opposition to Masonry and demonstrated an ability to live with the decision of the General Synod of 1870.

In view of the immensity of the eruption over Masonry in 1880, it is strange that this bitter disruption had not occurred in 1868-1870 when the issue first reached the synodical level and before the immigrant churches in the Middle West had adapted still more to the American scene. Apparently the difference was the living presence of Van Raalte himself. Although he had retired from his pastorate at the First Reformed Church of Holland in 1867, he remained active in the affairs of the Classis of Holland and the Particular Synod of Chicago. He also encouraged further Dutch immigration to North America, such as the unsuccessful colony in Amelia, Virginia, settled between 1868 and 1871, that he led for a time. Van Raalte remained the titular leader of the Dutch immigrant settlements in western Michigan until the time of his death on 7 November 1876. His very presence kept the lid on the simmering Masonic controversy and prevented it from boiling over as it did later, between 1879 and 1882.

The controversy simmered during the 1870s, and the discontent with the synodical actions of 1868, 1869, and 1870 never died out. In 1874 Gerrit Van Schelven, the astute editor of the *Holland City News* and a leader in the Holland community, reported that the First Reformed Church, Van Raalte's former congregation, had discovered two Masons in its membership. The editor then went on to say disconsolately that "this is the beginning of an unpleasant controversy."[18] Van Schelven did not realize how prophetic he was. For there soon followed a series of unfortunate incidents which precluded a peaceful solution to the Masonry question over which the eastern and western churches were at great odds. And, after 1876, Van Raalte's moderating presence was gone.

About the same time, Hope College, the institution that Van Raalte had founded, and which had been so useful to the Dutch immigrant churches, began to suffer severe reverses due to the poor management of its financial

---

[17] Henry E. Dosker, *Levensschets van Rev. A. C. van Raalte, D.D.* (Nijkerk: C. C. Callenbach, 1893), 331.
[18] Gerrit Van Schelven, "Editorial," *Holland City News,* 23 May 1874, 4.

Hope College Collection,
Joint Archives of Holland

Philip Phelps

resources under the direction of its president Philip Phelps.[19] In 1878 Phelps was relieved of the presidency, and in the same year the General Synod declared that theological education, begun in 1866, could no longer continue at Hope College because of the poor financial base of the college. Training young immigrant men for the ministry of the midwestern churches was extremely crucial to the life of the RCA, but, in an effort to save the college, the General Synod jettisoned theological education. The immigrant churches regarded this action as a "Masonic plot." G. Henry Mandeville, an eastern RCA clergyman and secretary of the Board of Education of the RCA, was appointed provisional president of the college to guide the institution through its crisis. The question of membership in the lodge was raised with his appointment. Either because he was a Mason or because of the majority vote of the General Synod a decade earlier, the typical Dutch immigrant response to the crisis at Hope College was that Masons were at

19 Wynand Wichers, *A Century of Hope, 1866-1966* (Grand Rapids: Wm. B. Eerdmans, 1968), 108-111.

Courtesy of Jay Vander Meulen

Van Raalte Memorial Plaque at Pillar Church

the bottom of the problem![20] This simplistic conclusion indicated that Holland had become a fertile field for controversy.

To the great dismay of Van Schelven, who knew that Van Raalte would never have condoned the invitation, the First Reformed Church, which in April of 1879 had dedicated a beautiful black marble plaque to Van Raalte's memory, invited an ex-Mason, Edmond Ronayne, to lecture on the supposed

---

[20] This was reported in the *Holland City News*, 6 September 1879, p. 1. The charge was made by A. Feenstra in a letter in *De Hope* on 23 July 1879. For the most part, *De Hope*, the paper published by Hope College for the midwestern Dutch immigrant community, kept a very low profile during the Masonic controversy. Wichers (*Century of Hope*, 109) claimed that it was under orders not to publish "abusive" articles. This policy was quite different from *De Wachter*, because that publication and *De Grondwet* did everything possible to enflame the situation. In addition, Cornelius Doesburg, the editor of *De Hope*, was an alleged Mason, one of the two who were members of First Reformed Church. Ruth Keppel, a student of local history, said that Doesburg was a Mason (conversation with the author, 5 August 1980).

evils of Masonry.[21] Ronayne, who lived in Chicago, devoted all his efforts to fighting the lodge and had published a book against Masonry that same year: *The Master's Carpet, or Masonry and Baal Worship Identical*.[22] The title of the book left no doubt as to his position, and it was this book that led to an invitation to come to Holland in June 1879, to inform the members of the RCA about Freemasonry and reinforce what they already knew about its "evils." Since Ronayne compared Masonry with the Roman Catholic Church, he was sure to have a good audience in Holland. In the Dutch immigrant mind, there was little doubt that Freemasonry was worse.

The itinerant lecturer declared unequivocally that these two religious systems "must without question be the doctrine and worship of demons." But he focused on the evils of Freemasonry and not on "Romanism" while in Holland. Freemasonry, he claimed, conducted "abominable, wicked, degrading ceremonies." It was incomprehensible, he continued, how any respectable man could join a lodge in view of what the lodge stood for and in view of the similarity between ceremonies it conducted and the Baal worship reported in the Bible. Moreover, like Romanism, Masonry was a religious system that demanded "blind unquestioning obedience to all its laws, rules, and edicts, whether 'right or wrong.'"[23] Not only should laymen refrain from joining the lodge, but any clergyman who became a member should be suspended from the ministry. Ronayne's message was considered "gospel" by the Holland churches, and the smoldering embers that had burned for years now flared into a major fire.

The churches responded to Ronayne's challenge immediately by petitioning the Classis of Holland to take action. At that time, the two leading ministers in the classis, Rev. Roelof Pieters of the First Reformed Church of Holland, and Rev. Nicholas M. Steffens of the First Reformed

---

21 The event was reported by Gerrit Van Schelven in his editorial, *Holland City News*, 26 April 1879, 4. A month later Van Schelven editorialized on Ronayne's impending visit: "We see it announced in the city papers that there will be held an exposition of the secrets of Freemasonry, by Mr. Edmond Ronayne, in the First Reformed Church, on the 3d, 4th and 5th days of June next. If that man does it, he makes a perjurer of himself, and how a perjurer can get permission to pollute that church——to say the least—marks an epoch in the history of it. It is an astounding piece of news to us, and it seems very inconsistent with its previous history" (ibid., 31 May 1879, 5).

22 Edmond Ronayne, *The Master's Carpet; or Masonry and Baal-Worship Identical* (Chicago: Streich Brothers, 1879).

23 Ibid., vii, 69.

Holland Museum Collection,
Joint Archives of Holland

Western Seminary Collection,
Joint Archives of Holland

Teunis Keppel   *Roelof Pieters*

Church of Zeeland, the largest and oldest churches in the classis, were, fortunately, president and stated clerk, respectively. Had Pieters not died during surgery the following February, he would probably have been a conservative throughout the controversy. However, Pieters seems to have been irenic and reasonable in comparison with the contentious elder of the First Reformed Church, Teunis Keppel, who led the laity in the First Church of Holland and became the de facto leader of the congregation after the death of Pieters. Pieters's premature death at a crucial period in the burgeoning controversy was a great loss to the First Reformed Church, the Classis of Holland, and the RCA. Steffens, a moderate in the controversy, favored the General Synod position of 1870.

Beginning on 3 September 1879, at a special meeting before its regular fall meeting, the classis met to deal with petitions urging the congregations to take action against Masonry and to begin a new movement in the RCA against membership in a secret society. The committee on overtures and judicial business made its report at this meeting and set the course of action for the classis:

To your committee three communications were referred, out of which the following appears: The First Church of Holland feels itself called upon to contend with the evil of Secret Societies, also found in our denomination, and requests Classis to take suitable and effective measures to this end.

The Church of Fynaart finding that one of its members belongs to two of this [sic] Societies, viz. those of Freemasonry and Odd Fellowship [sic] is busied at present by means of Christian discipline to save that brother and to purify the Church, and requests that Classis, whose duty it is, to watch on [sic] the peace and prosperity of the Churches, and who have a general Supervising power in cases of appeal over the acts and proceedings of the consistories within their bounds, take into consideration the propriety of expressing itself in regard to this general deceptive evil.[24]

The congregation of North Holland called Freemasonry a great sin "which may not be tacitly forborn [sic] in the Church of God," but "on the other hand it admonishes against imprudent and unchristian action which would further the greater sin of contention and division."[25] Membership in a secret society was, in short, an evil, but schism was a still greater evil.

The Classis of Holland disliked Masonry as an institution, but the question was how to deal with it. The classis agreed with the 1870 decision of the General Synod that the consistory had the right to expel a member if, after a proper period of prayer and pastoral concern, he did not discontinue his membership in the lodge. The report of the overtures and judicial committee mentioned further problems, however. Because the denomination did not ban membership in the secret society wholesale, the consistories which disapproved of Masonry found it difficult to discipline members and cast them out of the church, for other consistories would gladly accept such individuals into their fellowship. In addition, the action of the General Synod prevented a "hearty fellowship in the denomination." That is to say, the Dutch immigrant churches in the West could not experience full fellowship in the denomination with the eastern brethren if membership in

24 Classis of Holland Minutes, 3 September 1879, 280-281. The unpublished minutes are in the Joint Archives of Holland, Western Theological Seminary Collection, Holland, Mich..
25 Ibid., 281.

the lodge was tolerated. Also, the Classis of Wisconsin thought it offensive to the conscience of the people who opposed Masonry to attend General Synod and receive Communion at the hands of ministers and elders who disagreed with them and who might even be members of the lodge.[26]

The vote of the Classis of Holland to memorialize General Synod again on the question of Masonry passed by a vote of sixteen to six. The minority of six, led by Steffens, disliked secret societies but maintained that the General Synod's position of 1870 was true to the Reformed-Presbyterian system of church polity. Since the majority view prevailed, a committee was appointed to prepare the new materials for presentation to the June 1880, meeting of the General Synod. Pieters was the chairman; Steffens and Peter Lepeltak, a moderate and a conservative, were the other two ministers; two elders completed the five member committee. Keppel was not appointed to the committee.

During the period between 3 September 1879 and 7-9 April 1880, when the committee reported, Pieters died, but a full report had been prepared for the classes. It took three major sittings for the classes to review the document and vote twenty-three to three in favor of the report. The conservatives had won, and 3,500 copies of the report were ordered and distributed to the churches before the meeting of the General Synod in June. During the same period, September to June, the entire midwestern Dutch immigrant community became involved in the controversy. When the General Synod convened in June of 1880, it had memorials not only from the Classis of Holland, but also from the Classis of Grand River (which included the Grand Haven and Grand Rapids RCA churches), the Classis of Illinois (which represented the American non-immigrant RCA churches in Illinois), and the Classis of Wisconsin (which represented the Dutch immigrant RCA churches of Illinois, Iowa, and Wisconsin).

The overture and memorial from the Classis of Wisconsin, by far the most articulate, was undoubtedly composed by Karsten, a veteran fighter against Masonry. It was deemed to be the most representative of the anti-Masonic overtures, so the synod dealt with it directly. The overture from Wisconsin included the usual diatribes against Freemasonry (e.g., that it was "the child

---

26   "A Memorial on the Subject Freemasonry to the General Synod of the Reformed Dutch Church in America to Meet in Brooklyn June 2nd 1880, Presented by the Classis of Wisconsin and Her Action of April 22d 1880." *Acts and Proceedings of the General Synod of the Reformed Church in America,...1880.* The attitudes toward Masonry were identical in the Classes of Holland and Wisconsin.

John H. Karsten

of darkness and communistic"), but the overture also included a novel theme: Freemasonry was "anti-Republican, anti-Christian, and anti-Reformed."[27] Masonry was clearly anti-Christian because it had no Savior and was universalistic in its approach to religious truth. It was anti-Reformed because it disagreed with the Heidelberg Catechism and taught another way of salvation than Jesus Christ. But the principal emphasis of the document was that Freemasonry was anti-Republican because it was "contrary to the spirit of American institutions." The Masons promoted political preferment of fellow members, a practice contrary to American democratic principles.

After the document concluded its doctrinaire position, it turned to a major problem facing the immigrant churches. If the General Synod did not reverse its decision of 1870 and take a position agreeing with the position of the midwestern immigrants, the midwestern church was severely threatened by a loss of members, not from the impending secession (which did take place) but from a loss of "the new Dutch immigrants from the Netherlands

27 Ibid., 534

General Synod, Dutch Reformed Church in America, 1884

coming now in large numbers [who] may unite with the 'True Reformed Church' [CRC] in this land instead of the Reformed Church." The RCA wanted the immigrants now coming to North America in such great numbers to unite with them and increase the borders of their kingdom in the Midwest and not to join the despised dissidents of that time, the CRC, now for the first time openly acknowledged as a threat. Nor was this an idle, politically inspired threat.[28] For through its publication *De Wachter*, the CRC was proclaiming openly that the RCA was an impure church and toleration of Masons was only the final sign of its degradation.

The General Synod of 1880 knew that there was much agitation on the question of membership in the secret society, so it took the overtures seriously and debated them at length. The outcome was the same as in 1870,

[28] The word 'dissident' is used in a derogatory manner here, but Henry Beets, *The Christian Reformed Church: Its Roots, History, Schools and Mission Work, A.D. 1857 to 1946* (Grand Rapids: Baker Book House, 1946), 81, also acknowledged that early members of his church included "some reactionary, over-conservative elements."

but this time the synod spoke to the issue clearly and directly in an attempt to show the classes in the West that it took the overtures seriously:

> No communicant members, and no minister of the Reformed Church in America ought to unite with or to remain in any society or institution, whether secret or open, whose principles and practices are anti-Christian, or contrary to the faith and practice of the Church to which he belongs. This Synod solemnly believes and declares that any system of religion or morals whose tendency is to hide our Savior, or to supplant the religion of which He is the founder, should receive no countenance from his professed followers. That this Synod also advises Consistories and Classes of the Church to be very kind and forbearing, and strictly constitutional in their dealings with individuals on this subject, and that they be and are hereby affectionately cautioned against setting up any new or unauthorized tests of communion in the Christian Church.[29]

This firm but irenic statement was the official position of the synod and would remain so in spite of repeated attempts of the same classes to reverse the decision in the 1880s and 1890s.

The decision of the General Synod is misleading, however, because it does not reflect the full debate that took place at the 1880 synod. The eastern majority was fully Americanized in its attitudes toward Masonry and lost patience with the minority of the delegates from the West. Dr. Elbert S. Porter of the Williamsburgh, New York, Reformed Church, the leading spokesperson in the synod for the policy enunciated in 1870, was as articulate and firm in his defense of Masonry as Karsten, of the Alto, Wisconsin, Reformed Church, was in his attack. The words of Porter as reported in the Brooklyn papers typify the attitudes of the eastern RCA members at that time:

> I am a Mason; but being a Mason I am also a minister of the Lord Jesus Christ. I was born and educated in the Reformed Dutch Church; I have been a pastor of the church all the years since I was licensed to preach. I have never been out of the harness. I hope I am a Christian while I am a Mason, and a Royal Arch Mason of the

---

[29] *Acts and Proceedings of the General Synod,...1880*, 536.

Seventh Degree. I never believed there was an institution in the world superior to the Church to which I belong. My Christian brother (a member of the synod from the West) said that he would not belong to an institution which was not founded by God.[30]

Porter then made a joke out of his Christian brother's remarks by asking, "Was he a Democrat or a Republican?" The reporter of the Brooklyn paper reported that laughter followed that question. But since Porter did not want to seem flippant, he continued: "I belong to a lodge which meets on Court street [in Brooklyn]; nine-tenths of the members of my lodge are members of churches—ministers, deacons, elders, vestrymen, etc. The issue presented is, can we circumscribe the consciences of other people."[31] Throughout his extensive remarks, Porter simply expounded the traditional American understanding of the lodge membership as he and the church members he knew had experienced it.

The ruling of the 1880 General Synod (which basically affirmed the position taken in 1870) coincided with the minority opinion in the Classis of Holland, but the synodical decision solved no problems for the midwestern classes, particularly the Classis of Holland. The troubles increased. At the meeting of the Classis of Holland, 8-10 September 1880, the churches of the classis made clear their disapproval of the synodical decision. The synod still had not outlawed Masonry. At its 6 October 1880 meeting, the classes went on record that "public opinion has almost universally interpreted General Synod's actions as a decision that Masons were to be allowed in the communion of the Reformed Church." Synod, the Classis of Holland continued, had provided no help to consistories trying to "purify the church of this evil."[32]

A minority in the classis surely realized that synod's actions had been misconstrued, but most members of the Holland churches saw the issue in this light. The classis, clearly determined to show the member churches that it was opposed to the action of the synod (even though it could not do anything about it), went on record by a vote of seventeen to five as disagreeing with the action of the General Synod. Dissatisfaction and discontent were now rampant throughout Dutch immigrant churches of the

30 Newspaper clippings in the Archives of the RCA, New Brunswick, N.J.
31 Ibid.
32 Classis of Holland Minutes, 6 October 1880, 380-381.

Middle West, and the Classis of Wisconsin lodged a memorial against the action of the General Synod in its meeting of 20 April 1881.

Worst of all, not only were members leaving RCA congregations and joining the CRC, but they were not taking their membership papers with them, adding insult to the injury of secession and schism. Those congregations in the RCA that did attempt to discipline Masons often found that offending members simply left the RCA congregations which prohibited Masons and joined ones that did not. The primary example was right in Holland, where, despite the resentment of the Dutch churches, the Second [Hope] Reformed Church, founded by English-speaking Hope College faculty who had come from the East, accepted members of secret societies in its fellowship.[33]

The Dutch immigrant classes continued to press for action against Masonry in succeeding years, but the General Synod would never again discuss the Masonic issue in any detail. As a sop to the suffering churches in the West, the General Synod decided to meet in the West for the first time. It convened in Grand Rapids in June of 1884, at which time the delegates traveled to Holland to see Hope College and to take a large offering of $3,100 to build a home for the president of the college.[34]

In spite of repeated attempts to get the General Synod to change its mind, the focus of classical action was now simply to prevent wholesale secessions of RCA churches and members to the CRC. At the 21 October 1881 session of the Classis of Holland, the majority of members in the churches of Saugatuck and East Saugatuck, led by Rev. John C. Groeneveld, left the RCA.[35] Holland Classis met repeatedly that fall to stanch the exodus of members from the RCA: 7 September 1881, 21 October 1881, 2 November and 16-18 November 1881. At the 16 November meeting, the classis resolved once again to admit no Masons to membership in the classis but also resolved to stay with the RCA.[36] Yet at the same time the classis expressed its deep disappointment that the General Synod had not spoken more plainly on the "sinfulness of Freemasonry."

---

33 *Holland City News*, 10 June 1876, 5, reported that the Oddfellows Lodge was in charge of the funeral service for Alderman John Aling at Second [Hope] Reformed Church.

34 Wichers, *Century of Hope*, 112-113.

35 Classis of Holland Minutes, 21 October 1881, 469. East Saugatuck was called Fynaart at that time.

36 Classis of Holland Minutes, 16 November 1881, 493. Hope Reformed Church of Holland was a member of the Classis of Michigan and was not affected by the ban.

The next three sessions of the classis were occupied with Groeneveld's trial on the charge of schism. At the meeting of 18 January 1882 he was suspended by the narrow vote of nine to eight![37] This vote must be interpreted as a protest against the action of the General Synod. Keppel and Rev. Adrian Zwemer, who had risen to leadership in the classis, were among those who voted not to suspend Groeneveld. Here was a very divided classis; it was opposed to Masonry but barely had the heart to suspend a person who had seceded from the classis to demonstrate his dissatisfaction with synod's decision on Masonry.

After this vote, the Secession of 1882 began in earnest. At a meeting of the congregation of the First Reformed Church on 27 February 1882 the congregation voted eighty-six to eighteen to leave the RCA.[38] The Graafschap congregation and its minister, Zwemer, left the RCA the next day. To deal with the schism, the classis called a meeting for 1 March 1882 at the distinctive "Pillar Church" that housed the First Reformed congregation, but when the members arrived at the doors, Elder Keppel locked the church and refused the classis entrance. This was a harsh experience for a battered classis, but it was not so bad as the reports in the *New York Sun* and *New York Herald* that a major fracas had occurred at this church.[39] Instead, the classis adjourned peacefully and met at the nearby Third Reformed Church. A

---

[37] Classis of Holland Minutes, 18 January 1882, 532.

[38] As reported in the Classis of Holland Minutes, 1 March 1882, 545-548, a large majority of eighty-six men (since women did not have voting privileges at the time) at First Reformed Church approved breaking the ecclesiastical relationship with the Reformed Church. First Church consistory did not report that eighteen men opposed secession.

[39] *Banner of Truth*, the official publication of the True Reformed Dutch Church in New York and New Jersey, had little love for the RCA, but it did want to set the record straight: "The accounts which many, perhaps, have seen in the *Sun* and *Herald* of difficulties in the First Reformed Church of Holland, Mich., seems to have been exaggerated, and to be misunderstood by many—'A personal fist fight,' 'The Riot Act Read,' etc. The facts appears to be these: The members of that congregation at a public meeting, had voted 84 [sic] for and 18 against resigning their membership and connection with the Reformed Church. An extra Classis attempted to meet in the church-house, presumably to take possession and discipline the 84, among which were the consistory. The trustees refused to open the doors, and, of course, a crowd gathered around the grounds. After some wordy contention the Classis adjourned to another church to transact their business, and steps have been taken peaceably to effect the division of the church property. This is entirely distinct from the Christian or True Reformed Dutch Church in the West." *Banner of Truth* 16 (1881/82):159.

Private collection of Elton J. Bruins

Pillar (Ninth Street) Christian Reformed Church

major concern was how to shepherd the small minority that wanted to continue the existence of the First Reformed Church congregation as an RCA church.

The roll call of delegates for the 1 March 1882 meeting revealed a decimated classis. The stated clerk, Zwemer, had defected. Four congregations had seceded. Several churches were unrepresented. Yet one decision made at this unhappy session was to counsel the minority of the Pillar Church "not to resort to forcible seizure of the property." However, in the following year a legal battle was joined when the minority sued to regain the property of the church. The courts found against the minority, and thus the historic Pillar Church was lost to the RCA.[40]

The minority then erected a new building at the other corner of the same block on Ninth Street, but through the decades the cry has gone from one generation of RCA members to the next: "They stole our church!" The final

---

40 The record of this lawsuit is in the Joint Archives of Holland.

Interior of Pillar Christian Reformed Church

blow came in 1884 when the seceded congregation united with the CRC.[41] But after the loss of the First Reformed Church, the troubles subsided. The Secession of 1882 was over.

Certain conclusions can be drawn about the effects of the Secession of 1882 on the RCA. Although the RCA leaders in the Midwest tended to minimize the effect of the 1882 secession, it was far more hurtful and damaging to the RCA, especially its Dutch immigrant wing, than the 1857 secession had been.[42] The most injurious aspect of the Secession of 1882

---

[41] As bitter as the loss of the Pillar Church was to the RCA, the CRC gladly received that congregation into the fold. Said Beets (*Christian Reformed Church*, 81): "last but not least [in the number of congregations that joined the CRC during the controversy], December 3, 1884, the First Church of Holland, Van Raalte's old congregation, with its monumental 'pillar church,' was joyfully received into the Christian Reformed fellowship."

[42] Gerhard De Jonge, who aptly summarized the Secession of 1882 in an essay, "Secession Movements," stated that "the movement was not a success" (32), and that "the addition of more than a thousand members [to the Christian Reformed Church] was not to be despised" (33). This undated typed manuscript is in the Joint Archives of Holland.

was that the RCA lost the recognition of the mother church in the Netherlands, the Christelijke Gereformeerde Kerk in Nederland (hereafter CGKN), out of which Van Raalte, Scholte, and so many of their followers had come. From 1850 on, the CGKN had given its blessing to the RCA and, from 1857 to 1882, it had considered the CRC a dissident group that had lacked sufficient reason for seceding in 1857. The Masonic controversy changed all that. In 1882, the synod of the CGKN withdrew its blessing from the RCA and gave it to the CRC.[43] The long range effect of this action is incalculable, but it had to be considerable. After 1882, most of the new immigrants from the Netherlands joined the CRC instead of the RCA.[44]

The statistics of the CRC show the benefit of official recognition by the CGKN. In 1880, at the beginning of the Masonic controversy, the CRC had 4 classes, 12,201 members, 39 congregations, and 19 ministers. By 1890, it had grown to 7 classes, 37,834 members, 96 congregations, and 55 ministers. In 1900, the CRC numbered 144 congregations and 47,349 souls.

The CRC was clearly the beneficiary of the Secession of 1882. The RCA tended to minimize the rush of members to the CRC; Gerhard De Jonge, a leading RCA minister, concluded that only 1,000 members left the RCA, and RCA statistics for the Synod of Chicago show a net loss of 500 members between 1880 and 1884 when the great defections took place. The net loss appeared low because the RCA was also growing rapidly at this time, and its numerical recovery after the controversy was very rapid; and some members did return to the RCA, the most notable being Zwemer who brought his congregation back with him.

But the direct membership loss of 1,000 adults actually represented many more people, because noncommunicant members are not included in this tally. In actuality, at least one-tenth of the membership of the Particular Synod of Chicago, which represented the Classes of Michigan, Illinois, Holland, Grand River, and Wisconsin, was lost during the bitter controversy. The Classis of Holland alone had a loss of 1,622 persons between 1880 and

43 Beets, *Christian Reformed Church in North America*, 79.
44 Elton J. Bruins, "Immigration," in *Piety and Patriotism, Bicentennial Studies of the Reformed Church in America, 1776-1976*, ed. James W. Van Hoeven (Grand Rapids: Wm. B. Eerdmans, 1976), 70-71; Beets, *Christian Reformed Church in North America*, 73, mentioned that 85,517 Netherlanders came to North America between 1880 and 1900. The RCA statistics are found in the *Acts and Proceedings of the General Synod,...1880*, 532; and *Acts and Proceedings of the General Synod,...1884*, 499.

Calvin College Archives

Lammert J. Hulst

1884. Not many congregations left en masse as did First Church of Holland, East Saugatuck, Saugatuck, Fourth of Grand Rapids, and Graafschap, but eleven new CRC congregations were organized from individual members who left various RCA churches: Second of Grand Haven; North Street of Zeeland; Montague; Drenthe; Zutphen; Beaverdam; First Fremont; Spring Lake; Harderwijk of Holland; Overisel; and Alto, Wisconsin.[45] Of the ministers who left the RCA, the greatest loss was Rev. Lammert J. Hulst, who led the majority of members out of the Fourth Reformed Church in Grand Rapids and into the newly organized congregation of Coldbrook. By 1884, he was president of the Synod of the CRC and later the editor of *De Wachter*, the official publication of the CRC.[46]

It is also clear that if the CRC had not been organized in 1857, it would have been organized in 1882. By 1882 it was no longer possible to avoid a definite decision about what adaptation could be made to the American

45 Beets, *Christian Reformed Church*, 77-79.
46 Jacob G. Vanden Bosch, "Lammert Jan Hulst," *Reformed Journal* 7 (December 1957): 17-21.

scene. The CRC insisted that its policy was the safest and purest. Americanization was to be resisted as much as possible in denominational life. It saw accommodation to the American scene as a threat to its doctrinal position and its purity as a denomination.[47]

The Masonic controversy demonstrated clearly to the CRC that the RCA had failed to remain a pure church and that the Dutch immigrant congregations had compromised their souls by remaining with the RCA. Schism was clearly justified. Those in the RCA who regarded schism as the greater sin made their peace with the RCA and stayed within it. In spite of his leadership of the anti-Masonic faction of the RCA, Karsten never seceded, nor did the congregations he served in Wisconsin. Karsten and people like him stayed with the RCA grudgingly, for they could not see their way to foment schism. The Dutch immigrant churches that stayed with the RCA had Van Raalte on their side, and in time they had the great Reformed Church leader in the Netherlands, Abraham Kuyper, on their side, as well. In the 1890s, Kuyper adopted a position on Masonry similar to that of Van Raalte.[48]

After 1882, the RCA in the Middle West was forced to take another look at the young CRC, which was developing into a sturdy denomination and demanding at least a grudging respect. Bitterness between the two denominations endured well into the twentieth century, and ill feeling is still not entirely overcome. Still, by the 1880s the dissident group of 1857 had to be regarded as a full-fledged denomination in the very areas where the RCA had held sway, for in nearly every Dutch immigrant community in the Middle West a Christian Reformed church was erected, often only a short distance from the RCA congregation. After the Secession of 1882, the RCA took a self-congratulatory view toward the CRC, noting that the people who left the RCA brought new ideas and fresh air into the CRC and crediting them with reviving the Sunday school and the cause of missions in their new denomination.[49]

---

47 See Henry Zwaanstra, *Reformed Thought and Experience in a New World, A Study of the Christian Reformed Church and Its American Environment 1890-1918* (Kampen: J. H. Kok, 1973), for a thorough and scholarly discussion of the question of how the CRC handled the Americanization process during that period. The work by John H. Kromminga, *The Christian Reformed Church, A Study in Orthodoxy* (Grand Rapids: Baker Book House, 1949), is equally helpful on this subject.

48 Zwaanstra, *Reformed Thought and Experience*, 8.

49 One could expect such a chauvinistic attitude from someone in the RCA like Gerhard de Jonge, "Secession Movement," 33, who said, "Best of all, the new

Holland Museum Collection, Joint Archives of Holland

Vriesland Reformed Church

Western Seminary Collection, Joint Archives of Holland

Overisel Reformed Church

Western Seminary Collection, Joint Archives of Holland

Zeeland Reformed Church

Overall, the Secession of 1882 made clear the direction both churches were going to take. The RCA in the Middle West despised Masonry, but it

blood that entered the Christian Reformed Church in 1882, became the cause of liberation from the bondage of a sickly conservatism. Then their Sunday Schools began, then the spirit of Missions began to work, then higher education took its start. Then that Church began to be more liberal, lost its clannish exclusivism. Why the influx of the seceders of 1882 has all but swept away, every ground on which the secession of 1857 rested, and transformed that to such an extent that the fathers would not be able to recognize their church in the church of today." Beets, *Christian Reformed Church*, 81, essentially agreed with De Jonge: "This accession [of 1882] meant the infusion into the denominational body of precious life blood, that of a progressive element, with broader vision than some of the people of the older organization had ever had."

hated schism more. It would declare an uneasy peace with the denomination it had joined in 1850 and forge ahead. It hoped that more Dutch immigrants would join it even as it continued the process of Americanization as rapidly as feasible, despite the even more rapid loss of many Dutch-minded members. The CRC had finally won a place in the sun, and its future was assured. It now had its own school, its own publication, (*De Wachter*), and a clear policy for all Dutch immigrants; it would carry out the policies of the CGKN and adapt to the American way in a manner that would not endanger its doctrinal and ecclesiastical purity.[50]

50 Other useful works on the Masonic controversy and the Secession of 1882 are: *The Christian Intelligencer*; Henry E. Dosker, "In Memoriam," in Nicholas H. Dosker, *De Hollandsche Gereformeerde Kerk in Amerika* (Nijmegen: P. J. Milborn, 1888), vii-xv (published serially in *De Hope*, July 1882-May 1884); Roelof T. Kuiper, *A Voice from America about America* (1881), trans. E.R. Post (Grand Rapids: Wm. B. Eerdmans, 1970); and the personal papers of Albertus Pieters and John H. Karsten in the Joint Archives of Holland

Bibliographic Essay

The larger historical context of the religious turning points described in this book can be found in two comprehensive works: Jacob van Hinte, *Netherlanders in America: A Study of Emigration and Settlement in the Nineteenth and Twentieth Centuries in the United States of America* (1928), ed. Robert P. Swierenga, trans. Adriaan de Wit (Grand Rapids: Baker Book House, 1985); and Henry S. Lucas, *Netherlanders in America: Dutch Immigration to the United States and Canada, 1789-1950* (Ann Arbor: University of Michigan Press, 1955; reprint, Grand Rapids: Wm. B. Eerdmans, 1989). Van Hinte wrote from the Dutch point of view and analyzed the causes of migration, the process of transplanting, and the early growth of the American settlements with an emphasis on religious aspects. In contrast to van Hinte, Lucas, whose grandfather was among the pioneer settlers of Holland, Michigan, wrote from an American perspective. An interpretative social and religious survey that covers the entire sweep from the founding of New Netherlands to the postwar era is Gerald F. De Jong, *The Dutch in America, 1609-1974* (Boston: Twayne, 1975).

Archival Holdings

The official archives of the Reformed Church in America are in the Gardner A. Sage Library, New Brunswick Theological Seminary, New Brunswick, New Jersey. The Joint Archives of Holland are in the Van Wylen Library, Hope College, Holland, Michigan. The official archives of the Christian Reformed Church in North America are in the Calvin College Archives in Heritage Hall, Calvin College, Grand Rapids, Michigan. The extensive Scholte Collection is in the library of Central College, Pella, Iowa. The most complete materials of the New Netherlands immigration are at the New York Public Library and the New York Historical Society Library at Albany.

Primary Documents

The complete acts of the general synods of the Christian Seceded Church of the Netherlands are published in *Handelingen en verslagen van de algemene synoden van de Christelijk Afgescheidene Gereformeerde Kerk (1836-1869)* (Houten/Utrecht: Den Hartog, 1984). For the official minutes of the Hervormde Kerk synods, see *Officieele Stukken uit het Nederlandsch Herv. Kerkgenootschap* (Kampen, 1863). An English translation, in typescript, of the "Minutes of the Highest Assembly of the Christian Reformed Church, 1857-1880" is in the Calvin College Archives. The minutes of the Classis of Holland of the Reformed Church in America in the crucial first decade are published in *Classis Holland Minutes 1848-1858* (Grand Rapids: Wm. B. Eerdmans, 1950). An English translation by William Buursma of the minutes of the RCA Classis of Wisconsin, 1854-1865, are in the A. C. Van Raalte Institute, Hope College, Holland, Michigan.

Official RCA proceedings are: *A Digest of Constitutional and Synodical Legislation of the Reformed Church in America [Formerly the Ref. Prot. Dutch Church]* by Edward T. Corwin (New York: Board of Publication of the Reformed Church in America, 1906) and *The Acts and Proceedings of the General Synod of the Reformed Church in America*, 1820-1880. Accounts of participants in the early church struggles are in Henry S. Lucas, *Dutch Immigrant Memoirs and Related Writings*, 2 vols. (Assen, the Netherlands: Van Gorcum, 1955; reprint, Grand Rapids: Wm. B. Eerdmans, 1997).

Denominational Histories

An invaluable account of the growing unrest in the Nederlands Hervormde Kerk in the early nineteenth century is Gerrit J. tenZythoff, *Sources of the*

Secession: The Netherlands Hervormde Kerk on the Eve of the Dutch Immigration to the Midwest (Grand Rapids: Wm. B. Eerdmans, 1987). See also J. Vree, "De Nederlandse Hervormde Kerk in de jaren voor de Afscheiding," in *De Afscheiding van 1834 en haar geschiedenis*, ed. W. Bakker, O.J. de Jong, W. van't Spijker, L.J. Wolthuis (Kampen: J.H. Kok, 1984), 30-61. Other chapters in this book describe the Afscheiding of 1834, as does *"Van scheurmakers, onruststokers en geheime opruijers...": De Afscheiding in Overijssel*, ed. Freek Pereboom, H. Hille, and H. Reenders (Kampen: Uitgave IJsselakademie, 1984). Reenders's chapter, "Albertus C. van Raalte als leider van Overijssele Afgescheidenen," 98-197, is available in English translation by Elizabeth Dekker at the A. C. Van Raalte Institute. An analysis of the Afscheiding that draws parallels to a modern-day secession from the Christian Reformed Church is *The Reformation of 1834: Essays in Commemoration of the Act of Secession and Return*, ed. Peter Y. De Jong and Nelson Kloosterman (Orange City, Ia.: Pluim Publishing, 1984).

The story of the German Reformed Church of Graafschap Bentheim is told by H. Beuker, *Tubantiana: Church-State Conflicts in Graafschap Bentheim, Germany* (1897), trans. Albert Hyma and Mrs. Peter Slenk (Holland, Mich.: Historical Library Committee, Graafschaap CRC, 1986); Swenna Harger and Loren Lemmen, *The County of Bentheim and her Emigrants to America* (Holland, Mich.: privately printed, 1990); and Herbert J. Brinks, "Germans in the Christian Reformed Church, 1857-1872," *Origins* 9, no. 2 (1991): 36-43.

A new and very readable interpretive history of the Christian Reformed Church in North America is James C. Schaap, *Our Family Album: The Unfinished Story of the Christian Reformed Church* (Grand Rapids: CRC Publications, 1998), which supplements John Kromminga, *The Christian Reformed Church: A Study in Orthodoxy* (Grand Rapids: Baker Book House, 1949), and D.H. Kromminga, *The Christian Reformed Tradition: From the Reformation Till the Present* (Grand Rapids: Wm. B. Eerdmans, 1943). A popular history is Marian M. Schoolland, *De Kolonie: The Church That God Transplanted* (Grand Rapids: CRC Publications, 1973).

There is no general history of the Reformed Church in America. For the first two centuries see Gerald F. De Jong, *The Dutch Reformed Church in the American Colonies* (Grand Rapids: Wm. B. Eerdmans, 1978), and for the later period, the valuable essays of John Beardslee III, James W. Van Hoeven, and Elton J. Bruins in *Piety and Patriotism, 1776-1976*, ed. James

W. Van Hoeven (Grand Rapids: Wm. B. Eerdmans, 1976). A popular history is Arie R. Brouwer, *Reformed Church Roots, Thirty-Five Formative Events* (New York: Reformed Church Press, 1977). *Origins*, an historical journal of the Calvin College Archives, 1983-   , edited by Herbert J. Brinks, is indispensable. Scholarly analyses of Reformed intellectual movements are: Henry Zwaanstra, *Reformed Thought and Experience in a New World: A Study of the Christian Reformed Church and its American Environment, 1890-1918* (Kampen: H.J. Kok, 1973), and James D. Bratt, *Dutch Calvinism in Modern America: A History of a Conservative Subculture* (Grand Rapids: Wm. B. Eerdmans, 1984).

For differing interpretations of the Secession of 1857, see for the RCA side, William O. Van Eyck, *Landmarks of the Reformed Fathers, Or What Dr. Van Raalte's People Believed* (Grand Rapids: Reformed Press, 1922); Henry E. Dosker, *Levensschets van Rev. A.C. van Raalte, D.D.* (Nijkerk: C. C. Callenbach, 1893); and Nicholas H. Dosker, *De Hollandsche Gereformeerde Kerk in Amerika* (Nijmegen: P. J. Milborn, 1888), vii-xv (published serially in *De Hope*, July 1882-May 1884). The CRC defense is presented in Henry Beets, *De Chr. Geref. Kerk in N.A.: Zestig Jaren van Strijd en Zegen* (Grand Rapids: Grand Rapids Printing Co., 1918), and an abridged English version, *The Christian Reformed Church: Its Roots, History, Schools and Mission Work, A.D. 1857 to 1946* (Grand Rapids: Baker Book House, 1946); and Roelof T. Kuiper, *A Voice from America about America* (1881), trans. E. R. Post (Grand Rapids: Wm. B. Eerdmans, 1970). An English translation in typescript of Beets's 1918 book is in the Calvin College Archives. The account of a major participant is Gysbert Haan, *Voice of One Slandered* (1871), translation by William K. Reinsma and available in typescript at the Calvin College Archives. See also R. John Hager, "Gysbert Haan, A Study in Alienation," *Reformed Journal* 13 (Nov. 1963): 7-10, 13 (Dec. 1963): 12-15, 14 (Jan. 1964): 15-18.

A review of interchurch relations between the CRC and its mother denomination in the Netherlands is Willem van't Spijker, "The Christian Reformed Church and the Christelijke Gereformeerde Kerken in Nederland," 365-369, in Peter De Klerk and Richard De Ridder, eds., *Perspectives on the Christian Reformed Church: Studies in Its History, Theology, and Ecumenicity* (Grand Rapids: Baker Book House, 1983). The transatlantic nature of Dutch religious history is explained cogently in Herbert J. Brinks, "Religious Continuities in Europe and the New World,"

209-223, in *The Dutch in America: Immigration, Settlement, and Cultural Change*, ed. Robert P. Swierenga (New Brunswick, N.J.: Rutgers University Press, 1985).

Biographies

A multivolume biography in Dutch of the major Afscheiding leaders is J.A. Wormser, *Een Schat in aarden vaten:* Vol. I, *In twee werelddeelen: Het leven van Albertus Christiaan van Raalte* (Nijverdal: E.J. Bosch, 1915); Vol. II, *"Door kwaar gerucht en goed gerucht": Het leven van Hendrik Peter Scholte* (Nijverdal: E.J. Bosch, 1915); Vol. III, *"Werken zoolang het dag is": Het leven van Hendrik de Cock* (Nijverdal: E.J. Bosch, 1915); Vol. IV, *Karacter en genade: Het leven van Simon van Velzen* (Nijverdal: E.J. Bosch, 1915); J.C. Rullmann, Vol. V, *Ernst en vrede: Het leven van Georg Frans Gezelle Meerburg* (Baarn: E.J. Bosch, 1919).

A brief popular account in English of Hendrik de Cock, the father of the Afscheiding, is I. Van Dellen, *The Secession of 1834: A Reformation Movement* (Grand Rapids: Eerdmans, 1934). Albert Hyma, *Albertus C. Van Raalte and His Dutch Settlements in the United States* (Grand Rapids: Eerdmans, 1947), first utilized the long-closed Van Raalte collection. A full-length biography by Henry Dosker, *Levenschets van Rev. A.C. van Raalte, D.D.* (Nijkerk: C.C. Callenbach, 1893), is available in English typescript by Elisabeth Dekker at the A.C. Van Raalte Institute. A recent work that places Van Raalte and the Holland colony in the broader story of the nation is Jeanne M. Jacobson, Elton J. Bruins, and Larry J. Wagenaar, *Albertus C. Van Raalte: Dutch Leader and American Patriot* (Holland: Hope College, 1997). Van Raalte's sermon notes are described in Gordon J. Spykman, *Pioneer Preacher Albertus Christiaan Van Raalte* (Grand Rapids: Calvin College and Seminary, 1976). Lubbertus Oostendorp, *H.P. Scholte: Leader of the Secession of 1834 and Founder of Pella* (Franeker: T. Wever, 1964) is especially strong on Scholte's life in the Netherlands but the Pella years are sketchy. Jelle Ypma wrote the story of his ancestor, *Ds. Marten Annes Ypma, 1810-1863. Van Minnertsga (Friesland) naar Vriesland (Michigan)* (Leeuwarden: Gereformeerde Kerk, Hallum, and *Friesch Dagblad*, 1986). The biography of a founding church elder is told by Henry Beets, in *Life and Times of Jannes Van de Luyster, Founder of Zeeland, Michigan* (Zeeland, Mich.: Zeeland Record Company, 1949).

Sources of Illustrations

National Synod of Dortrecht, 1618-1619, page 8
Source: J.H. Donner and S.A. van den Hoorn, *Acta of Handelingen der Nationale Synode, . . . te Dordrecht, ten jare 1618 en 1619* (Leiden: D. Donner, n.d.), facing title page.

Bishop Simon Episcopius (1583-1643), page 9
Source: J.A. Gerth van Wijk, *Geschiedenis van het Protestantisme, naar J.A. Wylie, voor Nederlands volk* (Leiden: A.W. Sijthoff, 1887), facing page 583.

Willem I (1772-1843), King of the Netherlands (1813-1840), page 11
Source: J.A. Wormser, *Een Schat in aarden vaten*, III "*Werken zoolang het dag is:*" *Het leven van Hendrik de Cock*, (Nijverdal: E.J. Bosch Jbzn., 1915), facing page 28.

Official Dutch Psalter of 1777, page 13
Source: *Origins* 16, no. 1 (1998): 18.

Seceder "House Church," ca. 1835, Province of Gelderland, page 14
Source: J.C. van der Does, *De Afscheiding in haar wording en beginperiode* (Delft: W.D. Meinema, 1934), facing page 64.

Willem Bilderdijk (1756-1832), page 15
Source: G. Keizer, *De Afscheiding van 1834* (Kampen: J.H. Kok, 1934), facing page 65.

Isaac da Costa (1798-1860), page 15

Source: G. Keizer, *De Afscheiding van 1834* (Kampen: J.H. Kok, 1934), facing page 65.

Abraham Capadose (1795-1874), page 15
Source: G. Keizer, *De Afscheiding van 1834* (Kampen: J.H. Kok, 1934), facing page 64.

Guillaume Groen van Prinsterer (1801-1876), page 15
Source: G. Keizer, *De Afscheiding van 1834* (Kampen: J.H. Kok, 1934), facing page 65.

Petrus Hofstede de Groot (1802-1886), page 16
Source: J. van den Berg, P.L. Schram, and S.L. Verheus, eds., *Aspecten van het Reveil* (Kampen: J.H. Kok, 1980), facing page 32.

Hendrik de Cock (1801-1842), page 17
Source: Calvin College Archives

Exterior View and Pulpit of the Nederlands Hervormde Kerk at Ulrum, page 18
Source: G. Keizer, *De Afscheiding van 1834* (Kampen: J.H. Kok, 1934), facing page viii and facing title page.

Interior (restored) of the Nederlands Hervormde Kerk at Ulrum, page 19
Source: G. Keizer, *De Afscheiding van 1834* (Kampen: J.H. Kok, 1934), facing page 1.

Parsonage of Nederlands Hervormde Kerk, Ulrum, page 20
Source: G. Keizer, *De Afscheiding van 1834* (Kampen: J.H. Kok, 1934), facing page 176.

Hendrik P. Scholte (1806-1868), page 21
Source: Hendrik J.C. van der Does, *De Afscheiding in haar wording en beginperiode* (Delft: W.D. Meinema, 1934), facing title page

Members of the Scholte Club at the University of Leiden—
Anthony Brummelkamp (1811-1888), Simon van Velzen (1809-1896), Georg Gezelle Meerburg (1806-1855), and Albertus C. Van Raalte (1811-1876), page 22
Source: J.C. Rullmann, *De Afscheiding in de Nederlandsch Hervormde Kerk der XIXe Eeuw*, 2 vols. (Kampen: J.H. Kok, 1930), vol. 1, facing page 128 (van Velzen), page 136 (Meerburg); Van Raalte and Brummelkamp photos in Western Seminary Collection of the Joint Archives of Holland

Huibert J. Budding (1810-1870), page 25
Source: C. Dekker, *Huibert Jacobus Budding, 1810-1870: En zijn gemeenten in Zeeland* (Goes: Heemkundige Kring De Bevelanden, 1986), 11.

Hendrik P. Scholte, 1862, page 31
Source: J.A. Wormser, *Een schat in aarden vaten II, "Door kwaad gerucht en goed gerucht: Het leven van Hendrik Peter Scholte* (Nijverdal: E.J. Bosch Jbzn, 1915), facing page 216

Simon van Velzen as Professor at the Theological School at Kampen, page 31
Source: *Sola Gloria: Schets van de gescheidenis en werkzaamheid van de Theologische Hogeschool der Gereformeerde Kerken in Nederland* (Kampen: J.H. Kok, 1954), facing page 42.

Carel G. de Moen (1811-1879), page 32
Source: Western Seminary Collection of the Joint Archives of Holland

Anthony Brummelkamp (1811-1888), page 32
Source: *Sola Gloria: Schets van de gescheidenis en werkzaamheid van de Theologische Hogeschool der Gereformeerde Kerken in Nederland* (Kampen: J.H. Kok, 1954), facing page 16.

Jacobus Arminius (1560-1609), page 39.
Source: *Winkler Prins Encyclaepedie* (Amsterdam: Elsevier, 1948), 2:444.

Franciscus Gomarus (1563-1641), page 39
Source: W. van 't Spijker et al, *De Synode van Dordrecht in 1618 en 1619* (Houten: Den Hertog, 1987), 85.

Gisbertus Voetius (1589-1676), page 40
Source: A. Janse, *Van "Dordt" tot '34* (Kampen: J.H. Kok, 1934), facing page 32.

Gereformeerde Kerk, Ommen, page 42
Source: *Ommen 750, 1248-1998* (Ommen, 1998), 29.

Theological School, Ommen, page 42
Source: *Ommen 750, 1248-1998* (Ommen, 1998), 61.

John H. Livingston (1746-1825), page 44
Source: Edward Tanjore Corwin, *A Manual of the Reformed Church in America* (New York, 1869), facing page 143

Thomas De Witt (1791-1874), page 48
Source: Edward Tanjore Corwin, *A Manual of the Reformed Church in America* (New York, 1869), facing title page

Isaac N. Wyckoff (1792-1869), page 49
Source: Edward Tanjore Corwin, *A Manual of the Reformed Church in America* (New York, 1869), facing page 272

Cornelius Vander Meulen (1800-1876), page 51
Source: Holland Museum Collection of the Joint Archives of Holland

Marten A. Ypma (1810-1863), page 51
Source: *Vriesland Reformed Church 100th Anniversary, 1847-1947* (Vriesland, Mich., 1947).

Hendrik G. Klijn (1793-1883), page 51
Source: *Een Stem des Volks*, 31 May 1895, 2, in the Hope College Collection of the Joint Archives

Seine Bolks (1814-1894), page 51
Source: Western Seminary Collection of the Joint Archives of Holland

Settlers' Log Church, Holland, 1847-1856, page 52
Source: Holland Museum Collection of the Joint Archives of Holland

Albertus C. Van Raalte (1811-1876), page 52
Source: Hope College Collection of the Joint Archives of Holland

Zeeland First Log Church, 1848-1858, page 53
Source: *First Reformed Church of Zeeland Anniversary Book*, 9.

Graafschap Log Church, 1848-1862, page 53
Source: Graafschap Christian Reformed Church, Graafschap, Michigan

John Garretson (1801-1875), page 56
Source: Archives of the Reformed Church in America

Henry Beets (1869-1947), page 62
Source: Calvin College Archives

Walter A. Kok (1805-1891), page 70
Source: J.C. Rullmann, *De Afscheiding in de Nederlandsch Hervormde Kerk der XIXe Eeuw*, 2 vols. (Kampen: J.H. Kok, 1930), facing page 292

Jacob R. Schepers (1819-1878), page 70
Source: Calvin College Archives

Roelof H. Smit (1815-1886), page 72
Source: Western Seminary Collection, Joint Archives of Holland

Drenthe Scottish Church, 1853-1882, page 73
Source: *Drenthe Christian Reformed Church Diamond Jubilee Book, 1882-1957* (Drenthe, Mich., 1957), 9.

Original Drenthe Church, built in 1852, page 75
Source: Source: *Drenthe Christian Reformed Church Diamond Jubilee Book, 1882-1957* (Drenthe, Mich., 1957), 8.

Paulus Den Bleyker (1804-1872), page 77
Source: Local History Collection, Kalamazoo Public Library

Gysbert Haan (1801-1874), page 78
Source: Calvin College Archives

Koene Vanden Bosch (1818-1897), page 81
Source: Calvin College Archives

Noordeloos Christian Reformed Church, dedicated 1874, page 83
Source: Holland Museum Collection of the Joint Archives of Holland

Polkton Christian Reformed Church, Coopersville, Michigan, ca. 1858, page 86
Source: Calvin College Archives

Abraham Krabshuis (1815-?), page 89
Source: Holland Museum Collection of the Joint Archives of Holland

Graafschap Christian Reformed Church, dedicated 1862, page 92
Source: Holland Museum Collection of the Joint Archives of Holland

Niekerk Christian Reformed Church, organized 1866, page 92
Source: Calvin College Archives

Grand Rapids First Christian Reformed Church, page 93
Source: Local History Department, Grand Rapids Public Library

Holland (later Central Avenue) Christian Reformed Church (organized 1865), page 93
Source: Postcard in private collection of Elton J. Bruins

Douwe J. Vander Werp (1811-1876), page 96
Source: Calvin College Archives

Wilhelmus H. Van Leeuwen (1807-1882), page 96
Source: Calvin College Archives

Second Parsonage, Graafschap Christian Reformed Church, page 97
Source: *Graafschap Christian Reformed Church 150th Anniversary Book*

Philip Phelps (1826-1896), page 117
Source: Hope College Collection of the Joint Archives

Van Raalte Memorial Plaque, Pillar Church, dedicated 1876, page 118
Source: Courtesy of Jay Vander Meulen, Holland, Michigan

Teunis Keppel (1823-1896), page 120
Source: Holland Museum Collection of the Joint Archives of Holland

Roelof Pieters (1825-1880), page 120
Source: Western Seminary Collection of the Joint Archives of Holland

John H. Karsten (1833-1914), page 123
Source: *First Reformed Church of Alto, 1855-1930*, 14

General Synod of the Dutch Reformed Church in America, 1884, meeting at Grand Rapids (photo of delegates in front of Second Reformed Church), page 124
Source: Holland Museum Collection of the Joint Archives of Holland

Pillar (Ninth Street) Christian Reformed Church of Holland, page 129
Source: Postcard in private collection of Elton J. Bruins

Interior of Pillar Christian Reformed Church, page 130
Source: Hero Bratt, ed., *A Book of Remembrance: Pillar Christian Reformed Church (Ninth Street Christian Reformed Church, Holland, Michigan, 1847-1984* (Holland, Mich., 1984), 16.

Lammert J. Hulst (1825-1922), page 132
Source: Calvin College Archives

Vriesland Reformed Church, dedicated 1869, page 134
Source: Holland Museum Collection of the Joint Archives of Holland

Overisel Reformed Church, 1866-1947, page 134
Source: Overisel Reformed Church, *Centennial of the Church Edifice*, Overisel, Michigan, 1966

Zeeland Reformed Church, dedicated 1867, page 134
Source: *First Reformed Church of Zeeland, 100th Anniversary Book*, 12

Index

Pella (Ia.) colony, 6, 59, 96
Pereboom, Freek, 24n, 138
persecution, of Seceders of 1834, 23-27
Phelps, Philip, 117 (photo)
Pieters, Albertus, 10n, 12n, 134n
Pieters, Aleida, 37n
Pieters, Roelof, 119-120, 122
Pillar Christian Reformed Church,
    Holland, Mich., 2, 109, 118- 122, 128-
    130; exterior photo 129; interior photo
    130
Pioneer School, Holland, 109
Plasman family, 68n
Plug, Peter, 78n
Plymouth Brethren, 28
Polkton (Coopersville), Mich., 84n
Polkton (Mich.) Christian Reformed
    Church, 86 (photo); disintegration of,
    91; and Secession of 1857, 82, 86-87, 90
Porter, Elbert S., 125-126
Prakke, H.J., 70n
premillenialism, 32-33
Presbyterians, 43, 47, 59
Psalms, issue of, 71n, 78
Psalter Hymnal, 3

Queen's College, 44
Queens, N.Y., 43

Rabbers, Jan, 91
Randstad, emigration from, 102
Raritan, N.J., 43
rational religion, in Netherlands, 8-10. *See
    also* Réveil
Reenders, H., 24n, 26n, 41n, 138
Reformed Bible College, 37
Reformed Church in America, 1, 3, 109;
    Americanization of, 2, 44, 88, 108, 125-
    126; character of, in 1846, 47; and
    Classis of Holland, 58-59; compared to
    Nederlands Hervormde Kerk, 47; criti-
    cisms of, 61-62, 84, 78-79; declares
    independence from Classis of Amster-
    dam; eastern wing, 67, 108, 112; and
    freemasonry, 2, 112-113, 122; General
    Synod of 1824, 46, of 1847, 85n, of
    1868, 113-114, of 1870, 114-115, 120,

122, of 1878, 117, of 1880, 124, 126,
    127; growth of, 59, 64; history of, 42-47;
    and Holland colony, 56, 61, 80;
    homogeneity of, 6; and Hope College,
    116-118; Isaac N. Wyckoff's church
    planting role in, 51-54; language change
    in, 43; membership losses in, 127, 131-
    132; membership profile of, 98-102;
    ministerial profile of, 102-103;
    Particular Synod of Albany, 57, 66, of
    Chicago, 116, 132, of Poughkeepsie,
    N.Y., 57; and Secession of 1834, 34; and
    Secession of 1857, 82; social issues in,
    112; theological transition in, 38; and
    union of 1850, 59-60; A.C. Van Raalte's
    knowledge of, 58
Reformed Churches under the Cross, 23,
    30, 80n. *See also* Gereformeerde
    Kerken onder het Kruis
Reformed Dutch Church. *See* Reformed
    Church in America
Reformed Protestant Dutch Church, 95.
    See also Reformed Church in America
Reinsma, William K., 78n, 139
Reid, Daniel C., 46n
religious life, eighteenth century, in
    America, 45
Restored Church of Christ, 13
"Return" of 1857, 61, 82
Réveil, 13-15, 21, 41, 76; links to Secession
    of 1834, 16; and millenialism, 15
Revolutionary War (American), 45
Ridott (Ill.) Christian Reformed Church,
    96
Rhineland, Germany, 47
Rhine River, 101
Rochester (N.Y.), Reformed churches in,
    77
Roman Catholics, in Netherlands, 6; and
    freemasonry, 112, 119
"Romanism," 119
Romeyn, James, 58
Ronayne, Edmond, 118-119
Roseland, Ill., 59
Rotterdam, 101
Royal degree of 1836, 23
Rullmann, J.C., 23n, 140